vegetarian barbecue cookbook

vegetarian
barbecue
cookbook

Mary Gwynn

WHITECAP
BOOKS

This edition published by Whitecap Books
For more information, contact Whitecap Books, 351 Lynn Avenue,
North Vancouver, BC, V7J 2C4

First published in 1998 by Merehurst Limited, Ferry House, 51–57 Lacy Road,
Putney, London SW15 1PR

ISBN 1-55285-186-9
Library of Congress Catalog Card Number: 97-69992

Editor: Bridget Jones
Design: Hammond Hammond
Photographer: Ken Field
Home Economist: Louise Pickford
Stylist: Suzy Gittins

Color separation by Bright Arts (HK) Limited
Printed in Singapore

NOTE
The recipes in this book have been devised so that they can be prepared in the time
it takes for the coals to reach the correct cooking heat. Some foods need to marinate;
check ahead when planning a barbecue.

CONTENTS

FOREWORD

I first discovered the pleasures of informal cookouts as a child, and I have enjoyed eating outdoors ever since. Those totally unsophisticated childhood barbecues were usually instigated by my father during outings in the countryside on cold wintry days. The menu invariably consisted of small baked potatoes, wrapped in foil and cooked among the hot ashes of a fire made of wood we had collected. When they were cool enough to handle, the potatoes were still wonderfully warming in my small, chilly hands. Of course, there were baked beans—heated in the opened can and served on toasted currant buns. This may sound an odd combination and it had its detractors at the time, but to me it was totally satisfying in terms of both food and setting. In fact, those adventures sum up the joys of cooking and eating outdoors, when the food seems to taste better as everyone relaxes and joins in the informal fun.

Since then, I have experienced barbecues around the world. They range from spirited gatherings on a beach in the South Pacific, where we grilled an Australian "barbie" on vast grills set over oil drums, to the "real thing" on my first trip to the United States of America, when friends in Connecticut grilled the biggest steaks that I had ever seen, which we ate poolside with ears of sweet corn.

In those days, barbecued food offered little other than steaks, hamburgers, and sausages, which, unless in expert hands, ended up charred to a crisp on the outside and unpleasantly raw in the center. Now, however, the barbecue has been liberated! More people are moving away from meat-based meals; there's also a growing interest in Mediterranean and Asian food—with the focus on sealing in flavors by grilling, roasting, and searing. Today, grilling has become a healthy, innovative method of cooking that also offers all kinds of possibilities for vegetarians.

The recipes in this book offer only an idea of the many versatile ways you can use the grill for meat-free eating. They're intended as inspiration for everyone who enjoys good food. I hope you enjoy cooking and eating them as much as I have.

Mary Gwynn

GETTING STARTED

CHOOSING YOUR GRILL

All grills are based on the same simple structure, with a bed for fuel and a metal grilling rack set over it. Beyond this, there is an ever-increasing range of styles and sizes.

First, consider how often you will use your grill, how many people you are likely to feed, and where you intend to cook. The following are a few common types; make sure the grill you choose is sturdy and comes with a grilling rack that is easy to remove or reposition.

Braziers

From the inexpensive three-legged version to a more upscale unit complete with hood, rotisserie, and air vent, a brazier is your basic shallow firebox on legs.

Look for a brazier that is sturdy, with strong, solid legs. Those with adjustable settings for the cooking rack, and air vents that open and close, will provide a certain degree of heat control. Some braziers come with windshields to shelter the coals and to help conserve the heat.

This type of grill is best for quick-cooking foods no more than 1½ inches thick.

Kettle or Wagon Grills

Designs vary, but these grills have adjustable hoods, which allow them to be used as an open grill, covered roaster, or smoker. When closed, the heat is reflected to speed up the cooking process and make it more even. This is ideal for cooking thicker foods or whole vegetables. Air vents on the lid and base help control ventilation. Many models have optional accessories such as attachable shelves and utensil hooks.

Portable Grills

Portable grills are best suited for cooking smaller foods. The most common portable grill is the hibachi. Named from a Japanese word meaning "firebox," these are small, inexpensive, and easy to carry to the beach or on picnics.

Other portable grills include small-scale covered kettles, as well as disposable foil grills that burn for an hour or so—suitable for one-time use only.

Gas and Electric Grills

Gaining popularity are the fast-starting, easy-cleaning gas grills, fueled by refillable propane tanks or by natural gas. The cooking temperature is easily controlled by adjusting the gas flame; ceramic briquettes or lava rocks replace charcoal briquettes. Gas grills offer year-round cooking with direct heat, or covered grilling for roasting.

FUELING THE FIRE

Standard charcoal briquettes are the most common fuel for grilling. They start easily and their uniform pillow shape distributes heat evenly. However, you must wait until the coals have burned down and have a coating of gray ash before grilling. These briquettes usually contain chemical binders and fillers that can affect the flavor of your food if used before they are burned down.

Hardwood lump charcoal is the top choice of many grilling enthusiasts. It burns cleanly and evenly and provides a long-lasting fire that is somewhat hotter than standard briquettes. Also, it is additive-free.

A third choice is natural hardwood such as mesquite, hickory, or oak. This may be the purest choice and the most fun, but it's also the most challenging. Logs or pieces of wood take a long time to burn down, and they provide inconsistent heat, which can cause uneven cooking.

For a wood-smoked aroma and flavor, add wood chips or chunks to burning briquettes. Try experimenting with such woods as mesquite, alder, hickory, oak, and fruitwoods to find the flavor you prefer. Be sure to read package labels; chances are the chips will need to be soaked and drained before using so they'll smoke, not flame.

LIGHTING THE GRILL

To determine how much charcoal you need, a good rule of thumb is to spread coals in a single layer that extends about two inches beyond your food. Once you've determined the amount, push coals into a mound to light. (If you want to grill for longer than one hour, you will have to add more coals during cooking.)

A useful tip is to line the grill's base with heavy foil to reflect the heat back up at the food. This also makes the grill easier to clean afterwards.

To jump-start the coals, try an electric starter or use liquid lighter fluid, jelly or wax-type (solid) starters, or a chimney starter. Whatever type of starter you select, read the manufacturer's instructions carefully. Wait about a minute after adding a liquid, wax, or jelly starter before igniting the coals. Never add more starter after the fire has started—and never use gasoline or kerosene to start your coals. Self-lighting briquettes don't require a fire starter; simply light them with a match to start.

Once ignited, standard briquettes take about 20 to 30 minutes to burn; self-lighting coals take 5 to 10 minutes. Coals should appear ash gray or, at night, glowing red.

GRILLING TIMES

A charcoal grill and an electric grill were used for testing the recipes in this book. Grilling times will vary widely according to size and type of grill, weather, quantity of food cooked, and heat of coal temperature. Be sure to check food often during grilling, and never leave the grill unattended.

GRILLING TIPS

■ To cook vegetables, consider using a long-handled hinged grill basket. It will hold vegetables in place and make them easy to turn. Oil baskets well.

■ If cooking small or delicate vegetables on the grill, line a small area with heavy foil and pierce it. This way, the vegetables will not fall onto the coals. Or, use a mesh grill rack sold especially for vegetables and foods that might fall apart.

■ When cooking food wrapped in foil parcels, use a skewer to pierce the foil in several places to let the flavor through.

■ Wooden or bamboo skewers are ideal for vegetables, as they do not split delicate items—such as mushrooms—as easily as metal ones can. Soak wooden or bamboo skewers in cold water for 15 minutes to prevent them from burning.

■ Use metal skewers for root vegetables.

■ Keep a spray bottle of water on hand, spraying as needed to reduce flare-ups.

■ Always keep the grill clean by scrubbing it with a wire brush after each use.

■ When finished grilling, turn off a gas or electric grill, cover, and close vents. If using a charcoal grill, douse the coals lightly with water.

■ Keep children away from a hot grill.

■ Place the grill on a level surface away from any combustible materials. On a deck, use a flame-resistant pad underneath grill.

■ Only grill in a well-ventilated area.

MENUS

With the exception of simple salads and plain rice, all the recipes for these menus are featured in the chapters that follow. The menus show just how imaginative grilled meals can be, suiting all tastes and occasions. Page references for the recipes are given in the index.

■ A SIMPLE SPRING BARBECUE
Grilled Asparagus with Parmesan
    and Pine Nut Dressing
Mixed Baby Vegetable Platter with
    Chili Mayonnaise
Garlic Herb Pizza Bread
A simple mixed-green salad
Lemon-Glazed Pears on Raisin Toast

■ A SUMMER FAMILY GATHERING
Roasted Tomato Crostini
Mushroom Carrot Burgers with Feta Cheese
Vegetable Satay
Char-Grilled Fennel, Zucchini, and
    Onion Rice
Arugula with Char-Grilled Red Pepper and
    Caramelized Shallots
Banana and Strawberry Kabobs
    with Sticky Toffee Sauce

■ A MIDSUMMER OUTDOOR DINNER
Baby Artichokes and Eggplants with Alioli
Eggplant and Mozzarella Rolls
New Potato and Shallot Kabobs with
    Cilantro Pesto
Patty Pan Squashes with Lemon
    Mustard Dressing
Grilled Bread Salad with Parmesan
    and Mushrooms
Grilled Peaches with Whiskey Mac Cream

■ A FALL BARBECUE
Garlic Mushrooms
Pumpkin and Celeriac Kabobs
Grape-Leaf Parcels with Feta and
    Marinated Olives
Roasted Plum Tomatoes with
    Garbanzo Beans
Potato and Onion Bread
Figs with Lemon Grass and Honey

■ A MIDDLE-EASTERN INSPIRED
BEACH BARBECUE
Herb-and-Ginger Cheese with
    Grilled Vegetables
Falafel in Pita Pockets
Sweet Potatoes with Quick Curry Paste
Couscous Salad with Grilled Vegetables
Cucumber and Walnut Raita
Naan or purchased Indian flat bread
Exotic Fruit Kabobs with Cardamom
    Rum Butter

■ A CASUAL BARBECUE
Char-Grilled Tomato and Pepper Soup
Avocado, Tomato, and Pepper Salsa
Tortillas with Corn and Avocado
Grilled Halloumi Strips
Patatas Bravas
A tomato and red onion salad
Peach and Blueberry Parcels

■ AN ASIAN-INSPIRED BARBECUE
Roasted Eggplant and Cilantro Pâté
Corn and Red Onion Kabobs
    with Sesame Marinade
Thai Spiced Mushroom Kabobs
Peking-Style Marinated Tofu Steaks
Cooked jasmine rice
Salad of exotic fresh fruits

Appetizers

These are the recipes I like to serve while the
main dish cooks. They keep my guests happy,
whetting their appetites and offering them just a
small sample of the treats to come.

CHAR-GRILLED TOMATO AND PEPPER SOUP

Time to prepare: 15 minutes
Time to cook: about 10 minutes

Serves 4

2 red bell peppers
1 green bell pepper
1 yellow bell pepper
1 pound plum tomatoes
1 large mild onion, halved
horizontally
2 tablespoons red wine
vinegar
1 garlic clove
1 ¼ cups ice water
salt and freshly ground black
pepper
ice cubes, to serve

Garnish
diced red onion
chopped fresh flat-leaf parsley

Gazpacho is a firm favorite with my daughters, who request it whatever the season and temperature outside. This is a version that I developed during a visit to Spain, where the intensely flavored vegetables from the local market needed little enhancement other than a brush of the local olive oil to keep them moist as they grilled.

1 Place all the vegetables on the grill rack; grill for about 10 minutes, turning often, until the skins are blackened. Place the peppers and tomatoes in a plastic bag and set aside for 5 minutes to allow the skins to loosen.
2 Peel and coarsely chop the onion. Quarter, skin, and seed all of the bell peppers; set the yellow pepper aside. Skin the tomatoes. Place the red and green peppers in a blender with the onion and tomatoes. Process until smooth. Add the vinegar, garlic, and water, and process again. Season to taste with salt and pepper.
3 To serve, place two or three ice cubes in each bowl; pour in the soup. Finely chop the reserved yellow pepper. Sprinkle each serving with yellow pepper, diced red onion, and chopped parsley.

Cook's Tip
Sieve the soup to remove the tomato seeds for smoother results. The soup may also be made in advance, then chilled. Stir just before serving. Serve as above, omitting ice cubes.

Nutrition facts per serving: 59 calories, 1 g total fat (0 g saturated fat), 0 mg cholesterol, 49 mg sodium, 14 g carbohydrate, 3 g fiber, 2 g protein.
Daily values: 36% vitamin A, 223% vitamin C, 1% calcium, 6% iron.

Adding the finishing touch to Char-Grilled Tomato and Pepper Soup

ROASTED TOMATO CROSTINI

Time to prepare: 10 minutes
Time to cook: 10 minutes

Serves 4

8 ounces cherry tomatoes

2 garlic cloves, skins on

1 small red onion, halved

4 large fresh basil leaves, shredded

salt and freshly ground black pepper

¹/₂ medium French baguette

4 tablespoons extra virgin olive oil

Grilling is a wonderful way to boost the flavor of the rather tasteless tomatoes found in many supermarkets—even those that come with the hopeful label "vine-ripened." Outside the short summer season when the tomato plants in my garden perform and produce fruit, I tend to buy cherry tomatoes when I want a really full tomato flavor for my dishes; they work well in this classic topping for crostini—Italian for "little toasts."

1 Place the whole tomatoes, garlic, and onion halves on the grill rack. (Thread the tomatoes and garlic onto wooden skewers if they are in danger of falling through the rack.) Grill for about 5 minutes, turning occasionally, until vegetables just start to blacken.
2 Skin and chop the tomatoes and onion; combine in a small bowl. Add the basil; season to taste with salt and pepper. Skin and mash the garlic in a separate small bowl.
3 Thickly slice the bread and toast it on the grill until both sides are golden. Drizzle olive oil on one side of each slice and spread with garlic. Top with the tomato mixture and serve.

Nutrition facts per serving: 264 calories, 15 g total fat (2 g saturated fat), 0 mg cholesterol, 298 mg sodium, 28 g carbohydrate, 1 g fiber, 5 g protein.
Daily values: 3% vitamin A, 21% vitamin C, 4% calcium, 9% iron.

CHARRED GREEN ONION BRUSCHETTA

Time to prepare: 15 minutes
Time to cook: 10 to 15 minutes

Serves 4

20 large green onions
1 red chili pepper
1 tablespoon sesame oil
1 tablespoon soy sauce
1 tablespoon honey
2 tablespoons chopped fresh cilantro
4 thick slices coarse-textured bread
1 garlic clove

I really love bruschetta, an Italian combination of an open-face sandwich and garlic bread that makes a superb appetizer or light lunch. In its elemental form, it is simply toasted bread rubbed with a cut clove of garlic and drizzled with olive oil (the best available). It can also be topped with all kinds of wonderful ingredients—grilled vegetables among the most successful. Green onions brushed with a little soy sauce and sesame oil, then cooked to a mellow, caramel-complemented flavor, bring an Asian twist to this Mediterranean favorite. Try to find extra large green onions, as they are easier to handle and do not fall apart on the grill.

1 Cut the green onions in half horizontally. Seed and finely chop the chili pepper. Mix the sesame oil, soy sauce, and honey; stir in the chili pepper.
2 Place the green onions on the grill rack; brush with the soy mixture. Grill 10 to 15 minutes, turning and brushing with the soy sauce mixture, until onions start to blacken. Remove from the grill rack and cut into 2-inch lengths. Mix with the remaining marinade and cilantro.
3 Toast the bread on the grill. Cut the garlic in half. Rub one side of each slice with the cut surface of the garlic and pile the green onions on top. Serve at once.

Cook's Tip
For a more substantial topping gently stir cubes of grilled tofu into the warm green onions; set aside to cool.

Nutrition facts per serving: 179 calories, 5 g total fat (1 g saturated fat), 0 mg cholesterol, 495 mg sodium, 28 g carbohydrate, 2 g fiber, 4 g protein.
Daily values: 12% vitamin A, 28% vitamin C, 5% calcium, 11% iron.

BABY ARTICHOKES AND EGGPLANTS WITH ALIOLI

Time to prepare: 15 minutes
Time to cook: 10 minutes

Serves 4

**8 ounces young baby artichokes
(the type that are eaten whole)**

8 ounces baby eggplants

**extra virgin olive oil, for
brushing**

Alioli

5 garlic cloves

8 ounces mayonnaise

**salt and freshly ground black
pepper**

lemon wedges, to garnish

Alioli, the Spanish version of aioli found in Southern France, is definitely for garlic lovers only. On consulting a chef, I discovered that ten cloves of garlic were added for every cup of oil! My version cuts the garlic by half, which seems a happy balance for grilled vegetables. Occasionally, I serve a full-strength recipe, which is superb with paella-style rice dishes.

1 For the alioli, crush the garlic in a bowl. Add the mayonnaise and beat well. Season to taste with salt and pepper; transfer to a serving bowl. Cover; let stand at room temperature.

2 Cut the artichokes and eggplants in half from tip to stem. Brush with a little oil. Place on grill rack; grill for 10 minutes, turning occasionally until vegetables start to blacken. Garnish with lemon wedges and serve with the alioli.

Variation

NEW POTATOES WITH ALIOLI: For a quick appetizer, simmer baby new potatoes in water until almost tender; drain. Grill for 5 minutes, until golden. Serve on wooden toothpicks with the alioli.

Nutrition facts per serving: 414 calories, 41 g total fat (6 g saturated fat), 53 mg cholesterol, 102 mg sodium, 11 g carbohydrate, 4 g fiber, 4 g protein.
Daily values: 3% vitamin A, 14% vitamin C, 3% calcium, 8% iron.

GARLIC MUSHROOMS

Time to prepare: 10 minutes
Time to cook: 15 minutes

Serves 4

**8 large flat open fresh
mushrooms, such as portobellos**

Garlic Butter
$^1/_4$ cup butter
2 garlic cloves
**3 tablespoons chopped fresh
flat-leaf parsley**
**few drops bottled hot pepper
sauce**
1 teaspoon grated lemon peel
**salt and freshly ground black
pepper**

Large flat open mushrooms, such as portobellos, are an excellent choice for grilling, as this incredibly simple treatment is demonstrates. I use chopped garlic in my garlic butter because I like the chewy little pieces that really burst with flavor when you bite them; mince the garlic if you are not such a fan. Serve lots of crusty bread to mop up the garlic butter.

1 Wipe the mushrooms and remove stems; set aside.
2 For the garlic butter, cream the butter until softened. Finely chop the garlic; beat the garlic, parsley, hot pepper sauce, and lemon peel into the butter. Season to taste with salt and pepper.
3 Place the mushrooms on the grill rack, stem sides down; grill for about 10 minutes, until blackened.
4 Turn the mushrooms over and fill the tops with garlic butter. Grill 5 minutes more, until the butter has melted and the mushrooms are tender. Serve at once.

Nutrition facts per serving: 119 calories, 12 g total fat (7 g saturated fat), 31 mg cholesterol, 153 mg sodium, 4 g carbohydrate, 1 g fiber, 2 g protein.
Daily values: 11% vitamin A, 11% vitamin C, 14% calcium, 7% iron.

GRILLED ASPARAGUS WITH PARMESAN AND PINE NUT DRESSING

Time to prepare: 15 minutes
Time to cook: 10 minutes

Serves 4

1 pound fresh young asparagus
a little olive oil, for brushing

Parmesan and Pine Nut Dressing
1/4 cup pine nuts
1 garlic clove, peeled
a little kosher salt or salt
4 tablespoons freshly grated Parmesan cheese
2 tablespoons chopped fresh flat-leaf parsley
4 tablespoons extra virgin olive oil
freshly ground black pepper

Asparagus is often served with rich buttery sauces, but its distinctive flavor is also excellent with a good olive-oil-based dressing. Grilling the asparagus spears also accentuates their flavor. Serve with crusty Italian bread to mop up any juices.

1 Trim the asparagus. Brush asparagus with a little olive oil; set aside.
2 For the dressing, place the pine nuts and garlic in a mortar with a sprinkling of salt. Use a pestle to pound the ingredients together until you have a smooth paste. Work in the Parmesan and parsley. Gradually add the olive oil a little at a time until you have a thick dressing. Add freshly ground black pepper to taste.
3 Place the asparagus on the grill rack; grill about 10 minutes, until tender. Turn the spears often and brush with a little more oil if they become too dry. Serve with the dressing.

Cook's Tip
For a fabulous pasta dish, cut up the asparagus and toss it with the dressing. Serve with hot freshly cooked tagliarini or desired pasta.

Nutrition facts per serving: 229 calories, 22 g total fat (3 g saturated fat), 5 mg cholesterol, 118 mg sodium, 6 g carbohydrate, 2 g fiber, 7 g protein.
Daily values: 8% vitamin A, 40% vitamin C, 7% calcium, 10% iron.

HERB-AND-GINGER CHEESE WITH GRILLED VEGETABLES

Time to prepare: 15 minutes
Time to cook: 10 to 15 minutes

Serves 4

4 ounces baby carrots
4 ounces baby fennel
4 ounces baby leeks
1 cup even-sized fresh mushrooms
2 tablespoons extra virgin olive oil

Herb-and-Ginger Cheese

1 cup soft cheese, such as medium-fat soft cheese, ricotta, or cream cheese
$^1/_2$ cup plain yogurt with no gelatin added
1-inch piece stem (crystallized) ginger
4 tablespoons chopped mixed fresh herbs such as chives, parsley, tarragon, and basil
salt and freshly ground black pepper
flat-leaf parsley, to garnish

1 For the herb-and-ginger cheese, place the cheese and yogurt in a bowl and mix well. Finely chop the ginger; stir ginger and herbs into yogurt mixture. Season to taste with salt and pepper.
2 Trim and scrub the carrots. Wash the fennel and leeks thoroughly. Wipe the mushrooms and remove stems. Cook the carrots in a saucepan of boiling water for 5 minutes, adding the fennel and leeks for the last 2 minutes. Drain the vegetables; plunge into cold water to prevent them from cooking further. Drain well.
3 Brush all the vegetables with olive oil. Place on the grill rack; grill for about 10 minutes, turning often, until golden and tender.
4 Transfer the vegetables to plates. Garnish with flat-leaf parsley and serve at once with spoonfuls of the cheese.

Variation

FRESH YOGURT CHEESE: Homemade fresh yogurt cheese makes another wonderful accompaniment for grilled baby vegetables, but it has to be prepared 24 hours in advance. The process is so easy that I feel it deserves to be mentioned, as the final cooking is quick and in the spirit of the book.

Prepare the cheese at least 24 hours ahead. Place 1 cup plain yogurt with no gelatin added and 1 cup crème fraîche in a bowl; mix well. Finely chop the ginger; stir ginger and herbs into yogurt mixture as in the main recipe. Season to taste with salt and pepper. Place in the center of a large square of double-thickness cheesecloth. Draw the corners together to form a bag and tie securely with string.

Place the bag in a colander, and place a bowl underneath the colander to catch any liquid. Refrigerate for 24 hours until the cheese is firm. Keep chilled until ready to serve.

Nutrition facts per serving: 230 calories, 13 g total fat (5 g saturated fat), 22 mg cholesterol, 155 mg sodium, 20 g carbohydrate, 4 g fiber, 10 g protein.
Daily values: 73% vitamin A, 17% vitamin C, 21% calcium, 11% iron.

GRILLED BEET WITH PEAR AND ARUGULA SALAD

Time to prepare: 10 minutes
Time to cook: 10 minutes

Serves 4

---

8 small cooked beets

2 tablespoons extra virgin olive oil

4 ounces arugula leaves

1 ripe pear

juice of ¹/₂ lemon

Walnut Cream Sauce

6 tablespoons crème fraîche or sour cream

1 teaspoon Dijon mustard

¹/₄ cup walnut pieces, finely chopped

2 tablespoons chopped mixed fresh herbs such as dill, chives, parsley, and tarragon

salt and freshly ground black pepper

Baby beets are sweet and tender when prepared this way. For the best flavor, buy beets that are packed without vinegar or acid.

1 For sauce, mix together the crème fraîche or sour cream, mustard, chopped walnuts, and herbs. Season to taste with salt and pepper. Cover and chill.

2 Brush each beet with a little olive oil. Season to taste with salt and pepper. Place on the grill rack; grill for about 10 minutes, turning occasionally.

3 To serve, arrange a bed of arugula leaves on each of four plates. Quarter and core the pear and cut into thin slices. Toss pears and lemon juice; scatter over the arugula.

4 Cut the beets into quarters and arrange on the leaves. Spoon a little sauce over salads and serve at once.

Cook's Tip

The beets may be wrapped in foil and cooked directly among the coals to avoid taking up precious space on the grill rack. Place each beet on a square of aluminum foil and drizzle with a little olive oil. Season and wrap each beet in foil to make a small package. Tuck the packages in among the hot coals; cook for 15 minutes. Continue as directed in main recipe.

Nutrition facts per serving: 237 calories, 18 g total fat (5 g saturated fat), 20 mg cholesterol, 138 mg sodium, 18 g carbohydrate, 4 g fiber, 3 g protein.
Daily values: 9% vitamin A, 20% vitamin C, 4% calcium, 7% iron.

ROASTED EGGPLANT AND CILANTRO PÂTÉ

Time to prepare: 15 minutes
Time to cook: 10 to 15 minutes

Serves 4

2 medium eggplants
3 tablespoons olive oil
$\frac{1}{4}$ to $\frac{1}{2}$ teaspoon cayenne pepper
1 teaspoon ground cumin
1 garlic clove, minced
juice of $\frac{1}{2}$ lemon
2 tablespoons chopped fresh cilantro
salt and freshly ground black pepper
brioche bread, toasted and cut into strips, or pita bread, to serve

This pâté is based on an eggplant dip that I was served in a restaurant. It came as a topping for tiny morsels of brioche toast and had a garnish of diced tomato, roasted red bell pepper, and chervil leaves. I have transformed it into a pâté, based on the Middle Eastern classic *baba ghanoush* (also called "poor man's caviar"), and I serve it on brioche toast. Grilling eggplant intensifies its wonderful smoky flavor until it is practically irresistible.

1 Cut the eggplants in half from stem to base. Slash the cut surfaces with a knife into a crisscross pattern. Mix half the olive oil with the cayenne and cumin, and brush over the cut surfaces of the eggplant.
2 Place the eggplant halves on the grill rack, cut sides up. Grill for 10 to 15 minutes, until blackened. Turn and cook the other sides until golden and the flesh is very tender. Scrape the flesh out of the blackened skins into a blender or mixing bowl. Process or mash until smooth.
3 Add the garlic; then gradually add the lemon juice and remaining olive oil with the motor running or while beating continuously by hand. Mix in the cilantro. Season to taste with salt and pepper and serve with the toasted brioche or pita bread.

Cook's Tip
This recipe works well with fresh mint instead of cilantro, and it can be transformed into a wonderful relish by adding 2 seeded and chopped tomatoes, 1 chopped red bell pepper, and a finely chopped red onion.

Nutrition facts per serving: 263 calories, 13 g total fat (2 g saturated fat), 20 mg cholesterol, 305 mg sodium, 33 g carbohydrate, 6 g fiber, 6 g protein.
Daily values: 2% vitamin A, 10% vitamin C, 5% calcium, 17% iron.

Kabobs

The idea that vegetarians always take second best at barbecues is certainly addressed in this chapter, which really shows the versatility of vegetables for creating a whole range of colorful, attractive kabobs. These skewered foods are far more interesting to cook and eat than most meat-laden kabobs.

CHERRY TOMATO AND GARLIC KABOBS

Time to prepare: 5 minutes
Time to cook: 10 minutes

Serves 4

2 yellow bell peppers
14-ounce can artichoke hearts
12 elephant garlic cloves
20 cherry tomatoes
16 fresh bay leaves
2 tablespoons olive oil
1 teaspoon dried oregano
1 tablespoon balsamic vinegar
salt and freshly ground black
pepper

These kabobs are definitely for garlic lovers—if you are not a garlic fan, use shallots instead. Look for elephant garlic in the supermarket; the flavor of the cloves becomes sweeter and more subtle as they cook. Serve these kabobs with an Italian bread, such as focaccia, to mop up all the juices.

1 Halve and seed the bell peppers; cut into 1-inch squares. Drain the artichoke hearts.
2 Thread the peppers, artichoke hearts, garlic, cherry tomatoes, and bay leaves onto eight skewers. Mix the oil, oregano, balsamic vinegar, and salt and pepper to taste.
3 Place the kabobs on the grill rack; brush with the oil mixture. Grill for 8 to 10 minutes, turning and brushing with the oil mixture, until the skins of the tomatoes are charred. Discard bay leaves; serve kabobs at once.

Cook's Tips
Most Italian cooks prefer using dried oregano to the fresh herb as it has a stronger, more distinctive flavor; however, if you find it overpowering, substitute fresh oregano or use thyme or basil instead. If you can find them, substitute 8 young baby artichokes (the type that are eaten whole) for the can of artichoke hearts.

Nutrition facts per serving: 154 calories, 8 g total fat (1 g saturated fat), 0 mg cholesterol, 136 mg sodium, 21 g carbohydrate, 4 g fiber, 4 g protein.
Daily values: 8% vitamin A, 319% vitamin C, 6% calcium, 16% iron.

Serving Cherry Tomato and Garlic Kabobs with strips of Garlic Herb Pizza Bread, see page 73

THAI SPICED MUSHROOM KABOBS

Time to prepare: 15 minutes
Time to marinate: 30 minutes
Time to cook: 5 minutes

Serves 4

| 12 ounces shiitake mushrooms |
| 3 garlic cloves |
| 1 teaspoon Thai red curry paste |
| 2 tablespoons chopped fresh cilantro |
| 1 teaspoon grated fresh gingerroot |
| 2 tablespoons light soy sauce |
| 1 tablespoon dark brown sugar |

Chili and Cucumber Relish

| 4-inch piece cucumber |
| $^1/_2$ red onion |
| 1 to 2 small red chili peppers |
| 4 tablespoons rice vinegar or cider vinegar |
| 1 tablespoon granulated sugar |
| 1 teaspoon salt |

Shiitake mushrooms work best for these kabobs, but if you can't find them, use medium fresh mushrooms instead. If you are vegetarian, make sure that the red curry paste you buy does not contain shrimp paste.

1 Wipe the mushrooms; cut the mushrooms into quarters and place in a bowl. Crush the garlic; mix the garlic, red curry paste, cilantro, gingerroot, soy sauce, and brown sugar. Pour the paste over the mushrooms; mix lightly. Marinate for 30 minutes.
2 For the relish, cut the cucumber into quarters lengthwise. Thinly slice the lengths into small wedge-shaped pieces. Finely chop the red onion; seed and chop the chili peppers. Stir the vinegar, granulated sugar, and salt together in a small bowl until the sugar dissolves. Add the cucumber, onion, and chili peppers, and mix well.
3 Remove the mushrooms from the marinade and thread them onto skewers. Place on the grill rack; grill for 5 minutes, turning frequently. Serve at once with the cucumber relish.

Nutrition facts per serving: 69 calories, 1 g total fat (0 g saturated fat), 0 mg cholesterol, 803 mg sodium, 15 g carbohydrate, 2 g fiber, 3 g protein.
Daily values: 1% vitamin A, 21% vitamin C, 2% calcium, 15% iron.

NEW POTATO AND SHALLOT KABOBS WITH CILANTRO PESTO

Time to prepare: 15 minutes
Time to marinate: 15 to 30 minutes
Time to cook: 15 to 20 minutes

Serves 4

1 pound even-sized new potatoes
8 ounces shallots
1 garlic clove
^{1}/$_2$ green chili pepper
3 tablespoons olive oil
1 teaspoon grated lemon peel
salt and freshly ground black pepper

Cilantro Pesto
^{1}/$_2$ cup fresh cilantro leaves
1 tablespoon walnut pieces
1 garlic clove
3 tablespoons olive oil

Potatoes and onions are perfect partners, featured together in dishes around the world. Shallots are used here, but the kabobs can also be made with quartered mild-flavored onions such as red onions. Use metal skewers, which conduct the heat to the center of the potatoes and ensure they cook through properly. I suggest marinating the vegetables for 30 minutes, but 15 minutes is acceptable if you are in a hurry.

1 Scrub the potatoes and cook in a medium saucepan of simmering water for 5 minutes. Add the shallots for the last 2 minutes. Drain the vegetables and peel the shallots.
2 Crush the garlic, seed and chop the chili pepper, and mix both with the oil, lemon peel, and salt and pepper to taste. Pour the mixture over the vegetables and marinate for 15 to 30 minutes.
3 Meanwhile, place the cilantro leaves, walnut pieces, and garlic in a food processor or blender. Process until smooth. With the motor running, gradually drizzle in the oil until the mixture forms a thick paste. Season to taste with salt and pepper; transfer to a serving bowl.
4 Thread the potatoes and shallots onto metal skewers. Place the kabobs on the grill rack; grill for 15 to 20 minutes, turning occasionally and brushing with the marinade, until tender. Serve the cilantro pesto with the kabobs.

Cook's Tip
You can serve a purchased pesto instead of the cilantro pesto if you are short of time.

Nutrition facts per serving: 355 calories, 22 g total fat (3 g saturated fat), 0 mg cholesterol, 52 mg sodium, 38 g carbohydrate, 1 g fiber, 5 g protein.
Daily values: 73% vitamin A, 48% vitamin C, 3% calcium, 16% iron.

CORN AND RED ONION KABOBS WITH SESAME MARINADE

Time to prepare: 15 minutes
Time to marinate: 15 to 30 minutes
Time to cook: about 15 minutes

Serves 4

4 ears of fresh corn
4 medium red onions
2 cups broccoli flowerets
1 garlic clove
2 tablespoons olive oil
2 tablespoons teriyaki sauce
1 tablespoon sesame oil
juice of 1 lemon
salt and freshly ground black pepper
freshly cooked jasmine rice, to serve (optional)

Sesame oil is a full-flavored, fragrant ingredient to keep in every pantry. It smells wonderful when brushed over vegetables as they grill. Here, sesame oil adds its distinctive character to a simple marinade based on purchased teriyaki sauce. I suggest marinating the kabobs for 30 minutes, but this can be reduced to 15 minutes if you are in a hurry.

1 Remove the husks from the corn and cut each ear into four pieces. Cut the onions into quarters. Cook the corn and broccoli in a large saucepan of boiling water for 2 minutes. Drain and rinse under cold water; drain well.
2 Thread the corn, onion quarters, and broccoli onto skewers. Place the kabobs in a shallow dish.
3 Crush the garlic in a small bowl. Mix in the olive oil, teriyaki sauce, sesame oil, lemon juice, and salt and pepper to taste. Pour marinade over the kabobs and marinate for 30 minutes, turning occasionally.
4 Place kabobs on grill rack; grill for about 15 minutes, turning often and brushing with the remaining marinade, until the vegetables start to brown. Serve with freshly cooked jasmine rice.

Nutrition facts per serving: 212 calories, 11 g total fat (2 g saturated fat), 0 mg cholesterol, 461 mg sodium, 28 g carbohydrate, 4 g fiber, 4 g protein.
Daily values: 1% vitamin A, 25% vitamin C, 1% calcium, 5% iron.

SPICED ROOT VEGETABLE KABOBS WITH RHUBARB AND ONION CHUTNEY

Time to prepare: 10 minutes
Time to cook: 30 minutes

Serves 4

1 pound mixed root vegetables
such as carrots, parsnips, new
potatoes, and rutabagas
8 large green onion bulbs
1 tablespoon biryani paste or hot
curry paste
1 teaspoon tomato paste
2 tablespoons sunflower oil
salt and freshly ground black
pepper

Onion and Rhubarb Chutney
8 ounces rhubarb
1 medium onion
1 tablespoon sunflower oil
1 teaspoon mustard seeds
$1/2$ teaspoon ground turmeric
2 tablespoons raisins
$1/2$ cup cider vinegar
6 tablespoons brown sugar

A good-quality biryani paste is a useful ingredient to keep on hand, as it can be brushed over vegetables while grilling, as in this recipe. If you prefer a spicier flavor, use a good-quality hot curry paste. Serve these kabobs on a bed of rice pilaf or with the Couscous Salad with Grilled Vegetables on page 59.

1 For the chutney, slice the rhubarb and onion. Heat the oil in a small pan and add the onion. Cook for 3 minutes, until softened. Add the rhubarb, mustard seeds, turmeric, raisins, cider vinegar, and sugar. Bring to a boil and simmer, uncovered, for 20 minutes, until thickened. Transfer to a serving bowl.
2 Meanwhile, cut the root vegetables into 2-inch cubes; cook in boiling water for 5 minutes. Drain and rinse under cold water.
3 Thread the cooked vegetables and the green onion bulbs onto metal skewers. Combine the biryani or hot curry paste, tomato paste, and sunflower oil. Season paste mixture with salt and pepper to taste; brush over the vegetables.
4 Place the kabobs on the grill rack; grill for 10 minutes, turning often, until tender and golden. Serve at once with the chutney.

Cook's Tip
If you do not have time to make the chutney, serve a good-quality mango chutney instead.

Nutrition facts per serving: 278 calories, 11 g total fat (1 g saturated fat), 0 mg cholesterol, 73 mg sodium, 45 g carbohydrate, 6 g fiber, 3 g protein.
Daily values: 72% vitamin A, 40% vitamin C, 11% calcium, 22% iron.

PUMPKIN AND CELERIAC KABOBS WITH CINNAMON LIME BUTTER

Time to prepare: 10 minutes
Time to cook: about 20 minutes

Serves 4

12 ounces celeriac
3 cups pumpkin flesh
1/4 cup butter
1 tablespoon honey
grated peel and juice of 1 lime
1/2 teaspoon ground cinnamon
salt and freshly ground black
pepper

Halloween always tests my creativity for pumpkin recipes, as the house overflows with jack-o'-lanterns. I first discovered how well pumpkin and celeriac go together when I paired them up in a soup; the sweetness of the pumpkin is balanced by the cleaner flavor of the celeriac.

1 Peel celeriac. Cut the celeriac and pumpkin flesh into 2-inch cubes. Bring a medium saucepan of water to a boil, add the vegetables, and cook for 5 minutes. Drain and rinse the vegetables under cold water.
2 Melt the butter with the honey in a small saucepan and stir in the lime peel and juice, cinnamon, and salt and pepper to taste.
3 Thread the vegetable cubes onto skewers and brush with the butter. Place skewers on the grill rack; grill for 15 minutes, turning often and brushing with the butter mixture, until the vegetables are golden and tender.

Cook's Tip
Any combination of root vegetables will work well on these kabobs; for example, try sweet potatoes, rutabagas, and parsnips.

Nutrition facts per serving: 161 calories, 12 g total fat (7 g saturated fat), 31 mg cholesterol, 227 mg sodium, 16 g carbohydrate, 3 g fiber, 1 g protein.
Daily values: 61% vitamin A, 32% vitamin C, 5% calcium, 6% iron.

VEGETABLE SATAY

Time to prepare: 15 minutes
Time to marinate: 30 minutes to
1 hour
Time to cook: 5 to 10 minutes

Serves 4

1 pound firm tofu
1 medium carrot
1 medium zucchini
2 teaspoons ground cumin
4 tablespoons dark soy sauce
2 tablespoons red wine vinegar
2 tablespoons light brown sugar
Peanut Satay Sauce, optional
(see page 81)

Garnish
lime wedges
flat-leaf parsley

For classic satay, the chosen meat is cut into thin pieces, then marinated with sugar, spices, and a little soy sauce so it can cook through quickly without drying out. Here, strips of zucchini and carrot are wrapped around cubes of marinated tofu and served with the traditional peanut sauce to echo the classic flavorings. I suggest marinating the tofu for 1 hour, but this can be reduced to 30 minutes if you are in a hurry.

1 Cut the tofu into $1\frac{1}{2}$-inch cubes and place in a shallow dish. Mix the cumin, soy sauce, vinegar, and sugar; pour over the tofu. Cover and chill for 1 hour, turning tofu occasionally.
2 Just before serving, trim off the ends of the carrot and zucchini. Using a vegetable peeler, thinly slice strips off the carrot and zucchini, making thin ribbons. Wrap a ribbon of zucchini or carrot around each cube of tofu and thread onto metal skewers.
3 Place the kabobs on the grill rack; grill for 5 to 10 minutes, turning occasionally, until the vegetables are golden. Garnish with lime wedges and flat-leaf parsley and serve with the Peanut Satay Sauce.

Nutrition facts per serving: 88 calories, 3 g total fat (0 g saturated fat), 0 mg cholesterol, 308 mg sodium, 7 g carbohydrate, 1 g fiber, 8 g protein.
Daily values: 40% vitamin A, 1% vitamin C, 3% calcium, 11% iron.

EGGPLANT AND SMOKED TOFU KABOBS

Time to prepare: 10 minutes
Time to cook: about 15 minutes

Serves 3 to 4

1 large eggplant
8 ounces smoked tofu
12 fresh kaffir lime leaves or fresh bay leaves
1 teaspoon cumin seeds
2 dried chili peppers
3 tablespoons sunflower oil

To complement these cumin- and chili-seasoned kabobs, I suggest serving them with the Arugula with Char-Grilled Red Bell Pepper and Caramelized Shallots on page 62, or with the Peanut Satay Sauce on page 81.

1 Cut the eggplant and tofu into 2-inch cubes and thread onto bamboo skewers, alternating with the kaffir lime leaves or bay leaves.
2 Heat a small skillet; add the cumin seeds and chili peppers. Fry for 30 seconds, pour in the oil, and remove from the heat; leave to infuse for 5 minutes.
3 Brush the kabobs with the infused oil. Place on grill rack; grill for 15 minutes, turning often, until the tofu is crisp and golden and the eggplant has charred. Discard the kaffir lime leaves or the bay leaves. Serve at once.

Cook's Tip
If you cannot find smoked tofu, try marinating plain tofu instead. Mix equal parts of soy sauce and dry sherry, and pour over the cubed tofu. Marinate for 1 hour; drain and pat dry on paper towels. Use as above.

Nutrition facts per serving: 599 calories, 26 g total fat (4 g saturated fat), 0 mg cholesterol, 97 mg sodium, 100 g carbohydrate, 6 g fiber, 16 g protein.
Daily values: 96% vitamin A, 91% vitamin C, 82% calcium, 343% iron.

EGGPLANT AND MOZZARELLA ROLLS

Time to prepare: 15 minutes
Time to cook: 9 to 11 minutes

Serves 4

1 large eggplant
3 tablespoons olive oil
2 tablespoons sun-dried tomato paste
12 ounces mozzarella cheese
24 large fresh basil leaves
salt and freshly ground black pepper

These kabobs are similar in flavor to eggplant Parmesan, with an added smoky flavor from grilling. Watch the kabobs carefully during grilling, as the mozzarella can start to melt and get runny. Be ready to scrape off any that threatens to fall through the grill rack onto the coals.

1 Cut the eggplant lengthwise into eight ¼-inch slices; cut each slice crosswise in half. Brush the eggplant slices with half the olive oil. Place on grill rack; grill briefly for 2 minutes on each side until browned. Cool for 5 minutes.
2 Spread each slice of eggplant with a little sun-dried tomato paste. Cut the mozzarella into 16 strips and place one in the center of a slice of eggplant. Add a basil leaf and season to taste with salt and pepper. Wrap up to form a small package. Thread the packages onto four skewers.
3 Brush the skewered rolls with the remaining oil and place on the grill rack. Grill for 5 to 7 minutes, turning occasionally, until the eggplant is browned.

Nutrition facts per serving: 348 calories, 24 g total fat (10 g saturated fat), 48 mg cholesterol, 442 mg sodium, 12 g carbohydrate, 4 g fiber, 22 g protein.
Daily values: 16% vitamin A, 9% vitamin C, 47% calcium, 5% iron.

Cheese, Beans, and Tofu

This chapter is a fairly eclectic mix of recipes, all based on cheese, beans, or tofu, and all convenient to make. They make excellent main dishes for barbecues, and I find them especially popular for children.

MOZZARELLA-STUFFED RADICCHIO WITH BLACK OLIVE RELISH

Time to prepare: 15 minutes
Time to cook: 7 to 8 minutes

Serves 4

4 medium heads radicchio
2 tablespoons extra virgin olive oil
4 ounces buffalo mozzarella cheese

Black Olive Relish
$^1/_3$ cup black olives, pitted
4 sun-dried tomatoes in oil, drained
1 shallot
4 tablespoons chopped fresh flat-leaf parsley
1 teaspoon capers
2 tablespoons extra virgin olive oil
salt and freshly ground black pepper

Radicchio has quite a pungent, bitter flavor which mellows and becomes sweeter when grilled. Use the round variety for this recipe, as it is easier to stuff.

1 Drop the radicchio heads into a saucepan of boiling water and cook for 2 to 3 minutes. Remove from the water with a slotted spoon and pat dry on paper towels. Brush with olive oil and let stand for 10 minutes.
2 Meanwhile, for the relish, finely chop the olives, sun-dried tomatoes, and shallot. Mix with the parsley, capers, olive oil, and salt and pepper to taste. Place the relish in a serving bowl and set aside.
3 Cut the mozzarella into four cubes. Carefully open the leaves of the radicchio and ease a cube of mozzarella into the center of each head. Fold over the leaves to enclose the cheese securely. Place on the grill rack; grill for about 5 minutes, until charred and wilted. Season to taste with salt and pepper and serve with the relish.

Nutrition facts per serving: 166 calories, 17 g total fat (3 g saturated fat), 5 mg cholesterol, 139 mg sodium, 2 g carbohydrate, 0 g fiber, 2 g protein.
Daily values: 7% vitamin A, 15% vitamin C, 4% calcium, 2% iron.

Cutting into freshly cooked
Mozzarella-Stuffed Radicchio
served with Black Olive Relish

PEKING-STYLE MARINATED TOFU STEAKS WITH PLUM SAUCE

Time to prepare: 10 minutes
Time to marinate: 24 hours
(optional)
Time to cook: 7 to 11 minutes

Serves 4

10 ounces tofu
1 teaspoon Szechwan
peppercorns
1 teaspoon salt
1 teaspoon grated fresh
gingerroot
$1/2$ teaspoon five spice powder
1 tablespoon honey
1 tablespoon rice wine or dry
sherry
1 teaspoon sesame oil
1 tablespoon light soy sauce

To Serve
6 green onions
4-inch piece cucumber
prepared or bottled plum sauce
8 Chinese pancakes

I love the flavors associated with Peking duck—the pleasing balance of sweet and sour pairs perfectly with the crisp and soft textures provided by the vegetables, pancakes, and sweet plum sauce. Here, tofu absorbs the flavors of the classic marinade and crisps well on the grill, so vegetarians do not have to miss this meal usually centered on duck. While I suggest marinating the tofu for 24 hours, this can be reduced or omitted when time does not allow for marinating.

1 Cut the tofu into four strips and place them in a shallow dish. Place the peppercorns in a dry skillet and fry them for 1 minute.
2 Use a pestle to grind the Szechwan peppercorns in a mortar. Then mix in the salt, gingerroot, five spice powder, honey, rice wine or dry sherry, sesame oil, and light soy sauce. Pour over the tofu; cover and marinate in the refrigerator for 24 hours, if possible.
3 Before cooking the tofu, cut the green onions into short, thin strips. Peel and cut the cucumber into similar-sized strips.
4 Remove the tofu from the marinade. Place on the grill rack; grill for 3 to 4 minutes on each side, brushing with the marinade, until golden. Remove from the grill rack and cut into thin strips.
5 To serve, brush a little plum sauce onto each pancake and top with tofu, green onion, and cucumber. Roll up and serve.

Cook's Tip
Szechwan peppercorns are available in good supermarkets and specialty Chinese stores. If you cannot find them, use black peppercorns instead.

Nutrition facts per serving: 46 calories, 2 g total fat (0 g saturated fat), 0 mg cholesterol, 99 mg sodium, 2 g carbohydrate, 0 g fiber, 5 g protein.
Daily values: 0% vitamin A, 0% vitamin C, 1% calcium, 5% iron.

GRILLED HALLOUMI STRIPS

Time to prepare: 15 minutes
Time to marinate: overnight
Time to cook: 10 to 12 minutes

Serves 4

1 pound halloumi cheese
1 lime
1-inch piece fresh gingerroot
1 garlic clove
3 tablespoons chopped fresh cilantro
3 tablespoons olive oil
salt and freshly ground black pepper

Halloumi is a Greek cheese that has a firm, pliable texture rather like mozzarella. However, because it does not melt and become runny in the same way, it holds its shape well when cooked. This makes it ideal for grilling. Though rather bland on its own, halloumi absorbs flavors well and is excellent with a well-flavored marinade such as the lime and ginger one used here. It is best to marinate overnight. Arugula with Char-Grilled Red Bell Pepper and Caramelized Shallots, on page 62, goes well with this dish.

1 Cut the cheese into eight thin slices and arrange them in a single layer in a large shallow dish.
2 Finely grate the lime peel and squeeze the juice. Peel and finely chop the gingerroot and garlic. Mix the lime peel and juice, gingerroot, garlic, cilantro, olive oil, and salt and pepper to taste. Pour the mixture over the halloumi. Cover and marinate in the refrigerator for at least 12 hours.
3 To cook the halloumi, remove the cheese from the marinade. Place it on the grill rack. Grill for 10 to 12 minutes, turning often and brushing with the marinade, until the cheese starts to turn golden.

Nutrition facts per serving: 393 calories, 34 g total fat (18 g saturated fat), 100 mg cholesterol, 1,295 mg sodium, 6 g carbohydrate, 0 g fiber, 16 g protein.
Daily values: 14% vitamin A, 5% vitamin C, 46% calcium, 5% iron.

SPICED RED BEAN KOFTAS WITH MANGO AND COCONUT CHUTNEY

Time to prepare: 20 minutes
Time to cook: 9 to 11 minutes

Serves 4

14- or 15-ounce can red kidney
beans, well drained

1 teaspoon garam masala

$^1/_2$ teaspoon ground coriander

$^1/_4$ teaspoon ground cumin

$^1/_2$ small onion

1 garlic clove

$^1/_2$ green chili pepper

2 tablespoons olive oil

salt and freshly ground black
pepper

Mango and Coconut Chutney

1 green chili pepper

4 tablespoons unsweetened
shredded coconut

4 tablespoons chopped fresh
cilantro

1$^1/_2$-inch piece fresh gingerroot

1 garlic clove

1 tablespoon fresh lime juice

1 small ripe mango

flat-leaf parsley, to garnish

Koftas are spiced Indian patties made from meat, dal, or vegetables. Made here with red kidney beans, they are ideal candidates for cooking on the grill. Serve them with the Mango and Coconut Chutney, a green salad, and plenty of Indian bread, such as naan, or soft flour tortillas.

1 Place the beans, garam masala, coriander, and cumin in a bowl. Finely chop the onion and garlic. Seed and finely chop the chili pepper.
2 Heat the oil in a small skillet and add the onion, garlic, and chili pepper. Cook for 3 minutes until the onion is softened. Add to the bean mixture. Season to taste with salt and pepper; mash the ingredients together thoroughly. Shape the mixture into 16 small balls and thread them onto small wooden skewers.
3 For the chutney, seed and roughly chop the chili pepper; place in a blender or food processor. Add the coconut, cilantro, gingerroot, garlic, and lime juice. Blend the ingredients to a smooth paste; then add salt to taste.
4 Peel the mango. Cut the flesh away from the pit. Cut into small cubes and place in a serving bowl. Pour the coconut mixture over the mango and mix well.
5 To cook the koftas, place the skewers on the grill rack; grill for 6 to 8 minutes, turning often. Serve at once, garnished with flat-leaf parsley and accompanied by the Mango and Coconut Chutney.

Nutrition facts per serving: 205 calories, 9 g total fat (2 g saturated fat), 0 mg cholesterol, 212 mg sodium, 30 g carbohydrate, 7 g fiber, 8 g protein.
Daily values: 20% vitamin A, 51% vitamin C, 3% calcium, 12% iron.

MUSHROOM CARROT BURGERS WITH FETA CHEESE

Time to prepare: 15 minutes
Time to cook: 18 to 23 minutes

Serves 4

1 medium onion
2 garlic cloves
3 cups fresh mushrooms
5 medium carrots
2 tablespoons olive oil
2 cups fresh whole wheat bread crumbs
3 ounces feta cheese
3 tablespoons chopped fresh basil
2 tablespoons chopped fresh thyme
salt and freshly ground black pepper
2 eggs

This burger mixture is based on a recipe from the *Moosewood Cookbook* by Mollie Katzen. I bought this wonderful cookbook on my first trip to New York over twenty years ago, when vegetarianism was in its relative infancy and seemed to be based entirely on lentils and nuts. The *Moosewood Cookbook*, with its imaginative salads, wonderful breads, and inspiring alternatives to meat-based dishes, became my first veggie bible. I still turn to it for ideas or to revisit old favorites.

1 Finely chop the onion and garlic. Wipe and finely chop the mushrooms. Grate the carrots. You will save time if you use a food processor for these steps.
2 Heat the oil in a large skillet and add the onion and garlic. Cook for 3 minutes, until softened but not browned. Stir in the mushrooms and cook for 5 minutes more.
3 Place the grated carrots and the bread crumbs in a large mixing bowl. Crumble the feta; add feta and mushroom mixture to the bowl. Thoroughly mix in the basil, thyme, and salt and pepper to taste. Beat the eggs and stir them in to bind the mixture.
4 Shape the mixture into four flat burgers.
5 Use a spatula to place the burgers on the grill rack; grill for 10 to 15 minutes, turning often, until the burgers are golden. Serve with a leafy green salad.

Cook's Tip
To freeze the burgers, place them on a baking sheet lined with waxed paper and freeze, uncovered, for several hours. Wrap tightly and label. Freeze for up to one month. To use, thaw thoroughly; then cook as above.

Nutrition facts per serving: 255 calories, 15 g total fat (5 g saturated fat), 125 mg cholesterol, 464 mg sodium, 22 g carbohydrate, 5 g fiber, 10 g protein.
Daily values: 199% vitamin A, 8% vitamin C, 14% calcium, 17% iron.

GRILLED GOAT CHEESE AND HERB FOCACCIA

Time to prepare: 10 minutes
Time to cook: about 4 minutes

Serves 1

1 small garlic clove
1 green onion
2 ounces fresh goat cheese
2 tablespoons chopped fresh herbs such as basil, chives, marjoram, and flat-leaf parsley
salt and freshly ground black pepper
1 piece focaccia, about 5 inches square
1 tablespoon extra virgin olive oil
1 ripe plum tomato

This is actually a glorified grilled cheese sandwich cooked on the grill, but it really is wonderful. Now that it is becoming easier to find excellent-quality specialty breads in supermarkets, this recipe is simple to prepare. I use a plain rosemary focaccia, but any flavored flat Italian bread will work well, including varieties with ingredients ranging from mozzarella and garlic to sun-dried tomato and herbs. Choose a soft fresh goat cheese for this recipe, which makes a good informal appetizer when cut into strips and eaten with the fingers rather than knives and forks.

1 Finely chop the garlic and green onion. Place garlic, green onion, cheese, and herbs in a bowl. Add salt and pepper to taste and mash the ingredients until thoroughly mixed.
2 Split the focaccia in half horizontally and drizzle olive oil over each cut side. Slice the tomato. Spread the cheese mixture on cut side of bread. Top with tomato slices and the other piece of focaccia. Press the top down firmly to flatten the sandwich.
3 Place the sandwich on the grill rack; grill for about 2 minutes on each side, until the cheese melts and the bread is golden and crisp. Take care not to let the bread burn before the inside is heated through. Serve at once.

Cook's Tip
You can try all kinds of fillings for the focaccia, but a cheese filling that melts works best. For example, try mozzarella and grilled peppers, or feta with black olive paste and artichokes.

Nutrition facts per serving: 494 calories, 32 g total fat (12 g saturated fat), 50 mg cholesterol, 472 mg sodium, 36 g carbohydrate, 4 g fiber, 18 g protein.
Daily values: 14% vitamin A, 29% vitamin C, 11% calcium, 8% iron.

CHAR-GRILLED PEPPERS AND NEW POTATOES WITH MELTING FONTINA

Time to prepare: 20 minutes
Time to cook: 20 minutes

Serves 4

2 large red bell peppers
2 large orange bell peppers
1¹/₂ pounds small new potatoes
3 tablespoons olive oil
1 tablespoon chopped fresh thyme
1 tablespoon grainy mustard
6 ounces Fontina cheese
salt and freshly ground black pepper
crusty bread or Garlic Herb Pizza Bread (page 73), to serve (optional)

The inspiration for this recipe comes straight from recent skiing holidays spent in the Haute Savoie region of France. Melted cheese dishes served with large amounts of carbohydrate in the form of bread and potatoes are the perfect comfort food for bruised and tired skiers. Here, the addition of sweet peppers balances the richness of this French specialty. The cheese must be melted at the last minute and spooned over the vegetables; I suggest using a heavy iron baking sheet or grill pan for this purpose.

1 Halve, seed, and quarter the bell peppers. Cook the potatoes in a medium saucepan of boiling water for 8 minutes; then drain.
2 While the potatoes are cooking, mix the olive oil, thyme, and mustard. Pour this mixture over the drained potatoes and let stand for 5 minutes.
3 Thread the potatoes and peppers onto metal skewers. Brush with any remaining oil mixture. Place on grill rack; grill for 10 to 15 minutes, turning often, until the potatoes are golden and the peppers browned. Slide the peppers and potatoes off the skewers and into a shallow serving dish and keep warm.
4 Thinly slice the cheese. Heat a baking sheet or large flat pan on the grill rack and place the cheese on the hot surface. As the cheese melts, scrape it off the sheet or pan and onto the vegetables. Serve at once with crusty bread or Garlic Herb Pizza Bread, to mop up the juices.

Cook's Tip
If you cannot find Fontina, use a cheese that melts easily and becomes quite runny so that it can be scraped off the sheet or pan, such as Emmental, Gruyère, or Gouda.

Nutrition facts per serving: 458 calories, 24 g total fat (10 g saturated fat), 49 mg cholesterol, 506 mg sodium, 47 g carbohydrate, 2 g fiber, 16 g protein.
Daily values: 43% vitamin A, 299% vitamin C, 22% calcium, 16% iron.

FALAFEL IN PITA POCKETS WITH TAHINI MINT DRESSING

Time to prepare: 20 minutes
Time to cook: 6 minutes

Serves 4

2 14-ounce cans garbanzo beans, drained
1 cup fresh whole wheat bread crumbs
2 garlic cloves
1 small red chili pepper, optional
1 stalk celery
2 green onions
2 teaspoons ground cumin
2 teaspoons ground coriander
$1/4$ teaspoon turmeric
2 tablespoons olive oil
salt and freshly ground black pepper

Yogurt Dressing
6 tablespoons plain yogurt
2 tablespoons chopped fresh mint
1 tablespoon tahini paste

To Serve
4 pieces pita bread
tomato and cucumber salad (optional)

These spicy little patties cook well on the grill and can be served as part of a satisfying appetizer spread. Try them with the Couscous Salad with Grilled Vegetables on page 59, Roasted Eggplant and Cilantro Pâté on page 21, and Grape-Leaf Parcels with Feta and Marinated Olives, opposite.

1 Place the garbanzo beans and bread crumbs in a food processor.
2 Crush the garlic; seed and chop the chili pepper if using. Cut the celery and green onions into short lengths. Add the garlic, chili pepper, celery, and green onions to the food processor. Process until smooth. Add the cumin, coriander, turmeric, olive oil, and salt to taste. Process again to mix.
3 Shape the mixture into eight small patties and chill for 15 minutes.
4 Meanwhile, for the yogurt dressing, gradually stir the yogurt and mint into the tahini. Season to taste with salt and pepper and set aside.
5 Place the falafel patties on the grill rack; grill for 3 minutes on each side, until golden. Warm the pita bread on the back or to one side of the grill; cut in half and open into pockets.
6 To serve, slip a couple of falafel into each pita pocket and drizzle in a little of the dressing. Serve at once, with a tomato and cucumber salad.

Cook's Tip
Because tahini tends to separate when stored, stir it well in the jar to combine the thick paste with the oil on the surface before measuring out the required quantity.

Nutrition facts per serving: 469 calories, 14 g total fat (2 g saturated fat), 2 mg cholesterol, 1,185 mg sodium, 71 g carbohydrate, 10 g fiber, 17 g protein.
Daily values: 3% vitamin A, 22% vitamin C, 17% calcium, 57% iron.

GRAPE-LEAF PARCELS WITH FETA AND MARINATED OLIVES

Time to prepare: 15 minutes
Time to cook: 4 to 6 minutes

Serves 4

6 ounces feta cheese
¹/₃ cup marinated black olives, pitted
1 garlic clove
1 teaspoon capers
2 tablespoons chopped fresh marjoram or basil
freshly ground black pepper
16 large grape leaves in brine, drained
2 tablespoons olive oil

A full-flavored cheese filling transforms grape leaves into a smoky treat. The leaves are very salty, so do not add any extra salt to the filling. I like to use marinated olives for this recipe and usually buy those packed in olive oil flavored with garlic and lemon.

1 Cut the feta into small cubes and coarsely chop the olives, garlic, and capers. Mix the feta, olives, garlic, capers, marjoram or basil, and plenty of freshly ground black pepper.
2 Rinse the vine leaves, pat them dry on paper towels, and place them together in overlapping pairs. Brush the leaves with olive oil and divide the cheese mixture among them, piling it neatly on the middle of each pair. Wrap the edges of the leaves to enclose the filling and secure with wooden toothpicks. Brush again with olive oil.
3 Place the parcels on the grill rack; grill for 2 to 3 minutes on each side, until browned. Remove the toothpicks and serve.

Nutrition facts per serving: 189 calories, 18 g total fat (7 g saturated fat), 37 mg cholesterol, 805 mg sodium, 3 g carbohydrate, 0 g fiber, 7 g protein.
Daily values: 5% vitamin A, 0% vitamin C, 19% calcium, 2% iron.

Vegetables

As you would expect, most of the recipes in this book are based on vegetables; however, these in particular serve as main dishes, since they are a bit heartier. Of course, it is also easy to mix and match recipes as you wish, serving them in a variety of combinations. For help matching recipes, see Menus (page 9).

MIXED BABY VEGETABLE PLATTER WITH CHILI MAYONNAISE

Time to prepare: 15 minutes
Time to cook: 12 to 18 minutes

Serves 4

4 tablespoons olive oil

2 tablespoons chopped fresh
thyme

2¹/₂ pounds mixed baby
vegetables such as zucchini,
artichokes, asparagus tips,
eggplants, baby plum tomatoes,
carrots, and parsnips

coarse sea salt

Chili Mayonnaise

¹/₂ to 1 medium red chili pepper

1 garlic clove

1 egg yolk

²/₃ cup olive oil

juice of ¹/₂ lemon

1 teaspoon paprika

salt and freshly ground black
pepper

Baby vegetables, char grilled and arranged on a large platter, make a wonderful centerpiece for a more formal barbecue. Serve with the chili mayonnaise and mop up the juices with chunks of an Italian bread such as focaccia. They can also be passed as an appetizer, with a bowl of extra virgin olive oil for dipping, or even tossed with freshly cooked linguine pasta and topped with a dusting of freshly grated Parmesan cheese to serve as a pasta course. If you choose the latter, leave out the chili mayonnaise and just drizzle with some of your best extra virgin olive oil.

1 Place the olive oil in a small pan with the thyme and warm the mixture gently for 2 to 3 minutes. Set aside to infuse.
2 For the chili mayonnaise, seed and finely chop the chili pepper. With a mortar and pestle work the chili pepper and garlic to a paste. Place the egg yolk in a bowl and beat in the chili paste. Slowly drizzle in the olive oil, whisking continuously, until the mixture thickens. Stir in the lemon juice, paprika, and salt and pepper to taste. Transfer to a small serving bowl and set aside.
3 Trim and wash the vegetables as needed, cutting any larger vegetables in half lengthwise.
4 Arrange the vegetables on the grill rack; brush with the infused oil. Grill for about 10 to 15 minutes, turning occasionally, until browned and tender.
5 Arrange the cooked vegetables on a platter; sprinkle with sea salt. Serve at once with the mayonnaise.

Nutrition facts per serving: 538 calories, 51 g total fat (7 g saturated fat), 53 mg cholesterol, 278 mg sodium, 20 g carbohydrate, 8 g fiber, 6 g protein.
Daily values: 19% vitamin A, 59% vitamin C, 6% calcium, 16% iron.

Brushing the grilled mixed baby vegetables with remaining thyme-infused oil

MUSHROOMS STUFFED WITH PINE NUTS AND OLIVES

Time to prepare: 15 minutes
Time to cook: 10 to 13 minutes

Serves 4

8 large open fresh mushrooms, such as portobellos
$\frac{1}{3}$ cup black olives, pitted
1 garlic clove
$\frac{1}{4}$ cup pine nuts
$\frac{1}{2}$ cup fresh white bread crumbs
2 tablespoons freshly grated Parmesan cheese
2 tablespoons chopped fresh parsley
1 tablespoon chopped fresh oregano
3 tablespoons olive oil
salt and freshly ground black pepper

Large flat mushrooms are easy to stuff, and when the filling is pressed in firmly, it is possible to turn the mushrooms without losing too much of the bread crumb mixture. Try to pick mushrooms that have not opened out too much. This way, the upturned edges will hold the stuffing in place. Another way to keep the stuffing from falling out is to line the grill rack with foil with small slits cut in it.

1 Remove the stems from the mushrooms, wipe the caps and set them aside. Place the stems, olives, garlic, and pine nuts in a food processor; process until finely chopped. Alternatively, finely chop these ingredients by hand.
2 Add the bread crumbs, Parmesan, parsley, oregano, and 1 tablespoon of the oil. Mix well and season to taste with salt and pepper.
3 Spoon the stuffing into the centers of the mushroom caps and press down firmly, smoothing the top of the stuffing.
4 Brush the top of each mushroom with some of the remaining oil and place on the grill rack, stuffing side down. Grill for 5 minutes; then turn the mushrooms very carefully and cook for 5 to 8 minutes more, until cooked through. Serve at once.

Nutrition facts per serving: 200 calories, 18 g total fat (2 g saturated fat), 2 mg cholesterol, 158 mg sodium, 8 g carbohydrate, 1 g fiber, 6 g protein.
Daily values: 1% vitamin A, 8% vitamin C, 4% calcium, 15% iron.

ROASTED BUTTERNUT SQUASH WITH ORANGE PECAN BUTTER

Time to prepare: 5 minutes
Time to cook: 22 to 25 minutes

Serves 2

1 butternut squash, about 1¹/₂ pounds in weight

3 tablespoons softened butter

grated peel and juice of ¹/₂ orange

few drops bottled hot pepper sauce

2 tablespoons chopped fresh flat-leaf parsley

salt and freshly ground black pepper

1 tablespoon finely chopped pecans

A variety of weird and wonderful squashes are available in supermarkets, and they are ideal for barbecues. Squash can taste rather bland, but when brushed with a flavored butter and cooked over coals, the sweet flesh is transformed into a delicacy. I have used the golden, pear-shaped butternut squash here, but you can substitute other varieties such as acorn squash. Serve this squash dish piping hot, with a mixture of wild and long-grain rice and a salad of bitter leaves.

1 Place the whole squash in a large saucepan. Pour boiling water over the squash and return water to a boil. Simmer for 10 minutes.
2 Place the butter in a small bowl and beat in the orange peel and juice, hot pepper sauce, parsley, and plenty of seasoning. Beat pecans into the butter.
3 Drain the squash and cut it in half. Scoop out and discard the seeds. Place the squash halves on the grill rack, cut sides down, and grill for 5 minutes. Turn the squash over and spread the flavored butter over the cut sides. Cook for a further 7 to 10 minutes, until the flesh is tender.

Nutrition facts per serving: 289 calories, 20 g total fat (11 g saturated fat), 46 mg cholesterol, 254 mg sodium, 31 g carbohydrate, 6 g fiber, 3 g protein.
Daily values: 185% vitamin A, 107% vitamin C, 9% calcium, 12% iron.

PATATAS BRAVAS

Time to prepare: 10 minutes
Time to cook: 38 to 39 minutes
(see recipe introduction)

Serves 4

12 large new potatoes

¹/₂ teaspoon paprika

Tomato Sauce

1 small onion

1 garlic clove

1 small dried red chili pepper

4 tablespoons olive oil

1 cup puréed tomatoes

¹/₂ cup dry white wine

2 tablespoons chopped flat-leaf parsley

salt and freshly ground black pepper

flat-leaf parsley, to garnish

This is a version of one of my favorite tapas dishes, encountered in Seville during my first visit to mainland Spain, when I fell in love with the country, its food, and people. Although the total cooking time is slightly over 30 minutes, the potatoes and sauce simmer simultaneously, so the dish can be cooked within 30 minutes.

1 Scrub the potatoes, place them in a saucepan of cold water, and bring to a boil. Cook for 10 minutes, until the potatoes are almost tender.

2 Meanwhile, for the tomato sauce, finely chop the onion and garlic, and crush the chili pepper.

3 Heat 1 tablespoon of the oil in a small saucepan and add the onion and garlic. Cook for 3 minutes, until softened, then add the chili pepper, tomatoes, wine, parsley, and salt and pepper to taste. Simmer for 20 minutes until thickened, stirring occasionally.

4 Drain the potatoes and rinse under cold water. Pat dry and cut each one into four wedges. Brush the potato wedges with the remaining olive oil and sprinkle with the paprika. Place on the grill rack; grill for 5 to 6 minutes, turning frequently, until golden all over.

5 Transfer the potatoes to a serving dish; pour the tomato sauce over them. Garnish with flat-leaf parsley and serve.

Nutrition facts per serving: 288 calories, 14 g total fat (2 g saturated fat), 0 mg cholesterol, 67 mg sodium, 33 g carbohydrate, 3 g fiber, 4 g protein.
Daily values: 19% vitamin A, 56% vitamin C, 3% calcium, 23% iron.

CHAR-GRILLED FENNEL, ZUCCHINI, AND ONION RICE

Time to prepare: 10 minutes
Time to cook: 10 to 15 minutes

Serves 4

| scant 1 cup basmati rice |
| 2 fennel bulbs |
| 2 medium zucchini |
| 1 large mild onion |
| 5 tablespoons extra virgin olive oil |
| 1 garlic clove |
| grated peel and juice of $1/2$ lemon |
| 2 tablespoons chopped fresh chives |
| 2 tablespoons chopped fresh flat-leaf parsley |
| 1 teaspoon ground cumin |
| salt and freshly ground black pepper |
| 5 or 6 small plum tomatoes |

I have used long-grain basmati rice in this recipe because the grains stay firm and separate when cooked, and it adds its own fragrant character to the finished dish.

1 Bring a large saucepan of water to a boil, add the rice, and cook for 10 minutes.
2 Meanwhile, trim the fennel and cut it into quarters. Slice the zucchini lengthwise, and thickly slice the onion. Brush the vegetables with 2 tablespoons of the oil and place on the grill rack. Grill for 10 to 15 minutes, turning regularly, until charred. If necessary, cook the fennel for a little longer.
3 Drain the rice and place it in a serving bowl. Crush the garlic and whisk it with the remaining oil, the lemon peel and juice, chives, parsley, cumin, and salt and pepper to taste. Pour this dressing over the rice and mix well.
4 Cut the vegetables into large pieces and halve the tomatoes; then stir them into the rice. Add more salt and pepper, if desired, before serving warm.

Nutrition facts per serving: 365 calories, 18 g total fat (2 g saturated fat), 0 mg cholesterol, 69 mg sodium, 48 g carbohydrate, 13 g fiber, 5 g protein.
Daily values: 3% vitamin A, 33% vitamin C, 5% calcium, 21% iron.

POTATO WEDGES WITH ROSEMARY AND GARLIC

Time to prepare: 10 minutes
Time to marinate: 30 minutes
Time to cook: 15 to 20 minutes

Serves 4

1¹/₂ **pounds even-sized waxy potatoes**
4 tablespoons extra virgin olive oil
2 large fresh rosemary sprigs
2 garlic cloves
salt and freshly ground black pepper

Here's an old favorite that I have adapted from the oven to the grill with great success. The potatoes are marinated for up to 30 minutes in olive oil, garlic, and rosemary. Pass the potato wedges with the Salsa Verde on page 85 before the main course. Or, serve them with char-grilled bell peppers and eggplants drizzled with a little balsamic vinegar.

1 Scrub the potatoes and cut them in half lengthwise. Cut each potato half into three thin wedges. Place in a shallow dish; pour the olive oil over the potatoes.
2 Chop the rosemary and mince the garlic; add to the potatoes with salt and pepper to taste. Toss well to thoroughly coat in the oil. Set the potatoes aside to marinate for about 30 minutes.
3 Remove the potato wedges from the marinade and arrange in a hinged grill basket to make turning easier. Place on the grill rack; grill for 15 to 20 minutes, turning often, until the potatoes are golden and tender. Brush the potatoes with any remaining oil as they cook. Serve at once.

Cook's Tip
When they are available, use small new potatoes for this dish. I usually thread them onto metal skewers to make them easier to turn on the barbecue.

Nutrition facts per serving: 298 calories, 14 g total fat (2 g saturated fat), 0 mg cholesterol, 47 mg sodium, 41 g carbohydrate, 1 g fiber, 4 g protein.
Daily values: 0% vitamin A, 43% vitamin C, 1% calcium, 14% iron.

PATTY PAN SQUASHES WITH LEMON MUSTARD DRESSING

Time to prepare: 5 minutes
Time to cook: 10 to 15 minutes

Serves 4

1½ pounds patty pan squashes
(buy a mixture of colors, if
possible)
grated peel and juice of 1 lemon
1 tablespoon grainy mustard
1 tablespoon light brown sugar
1 tablespoon chopped fresh
oregano
5 tablespoons olive oil
salt and freshly ground black
pepper
2 tablespoons black olives,
pitted
4 cups mixed salad greens

Like their close relation, the zucchini, these little squashes get very waterlogged when overcooked. Grilling them with a well-flavored sauce or, as in this case, an oil-based dressing, helps to avoid this problem. The dressing also acts as a basting sauce for the squashes while they are cooking. Patty pan squashes are also ideal for kabobs and stir fries. The Tomato Chili Relish on page 84 goes well with this dish.

1 Wash the squashes and thread them onto skewers. Place the lemon peel and juice, mustard, sugar, oregano, and oil in a screw-topped jar with salt and pepper to taste; shake well.
2 Brush some of the dressing over the squashes; place on the grill rack; grill for 10 to 15 minutes, turning often, until tender and browned.
3 Coarsely chop the olives; place in a bowl with the salad greens and toss with a little of the dressing. Arrange in the base of a serving bowl.
4 Remove the squashes from the skewers and toss them with the rest of the dressing until coated. Arrange on the bed of greens and serve at once.

Cook's Tip
When selecting patty pans, look for vegetables of a good, even color, with smooth taut skins that are free of surface blemishes.

Nutrition facts per serving: 207 calories, 18 g total fat (2 g saturated fat),
0 mg cholesterol, 184 mg sodium, 12 g carbohydrate, 3 g fiber, 2 g protein.
Daily values: 5% vitamin A, 30% vitamin C, 5% calcium, 6% iron.

SWEET POTATOES WITH QUICK CURRY PASTE

Time to prepare: 10 minutes
Time to cook: 15 to 20 minutes

Serves 4

1¹/₂ pounds sweet potatoes

Quick Curry Paste
1 tablespoon cumin seeds
1 teaspoon coriander seeds
¹/₂ teaspoon black peppercorns
1 tablespoon paprika
¹/₂ teaspoon cayenne pepper
1 tablespoon ground turmeric
1 teaspoon salt
2 garlic cloves
juice of 1 lemon
4 tablespoons plain yogurt
mango chutney, to serve
(optional)

I can think of no better way of cooking a sweet potato than over hot coals. The whole process is simplicity itself, and it intensifies the nutty flavor of the vegetable while cooking the outside to a crisp shell. For this recipe, simply slice sweet potatoes and brush with the wonderful spice paste. I often make up a jar of the paste and keep it in the refrigerator to use in all kinds of dishes.

1 For the curry paste, heat a small skillet for a couple of minutes over a high heat. Add the cumin, coriander, and peppercorns; cook for 30 seconds.
2 Transfer the roasted spices to a mortar and grind to a fine powder with a pestle. Work in the paprika, cayenne, turmeric, and salt. Add the garlic cloves and a little lemon juice and pound the mixture to a paste. Stir this paste and the remaining lemon juice into the yogurt.
3 Scrub the sweet potatoes and cut them into ¹/₂-inch-thick slices. Pour the curry paste over the slices and mix well until coated.
4 Place the sweet potato slices on the grill rack; grill for 15 to 20 minutes, turning often, until tender. Serve at once, with mango chutney.

Cook's Tip
This recipe also works well with other root vegetables such as potatoes, rutabaga, and turnips.

Nutrition facts per serving: 171 calories, 1 g total fat (0 g saturated fat), 0 mg cholesterol, 561 mg sodium, 38 g carbohydrate, 5 g fiber, 4 g protein.
Daily values: 300% vitamin A, 70% vitamin C, 8% calcium, 19% iron.

TORTILLAS WITH CORN AND AVOCADO

Time to prepare: 15 to 20 minutes
Time to marinate: 1 hour,
optional
Time to cook: 12 to 15 minutes

Serves 4

4 ears of fresh corn
2 tablespoons tomato catsup
2 tablespoons vegetarian
Worcestershire sauce
few drops bottled hot pepper
sauce
2 tablespoons light brown sugar
juice of $1/2$ lime
1 red onion
$1/2$ green bell pepper
2 large avocados
4 flour tortillas
2 tablespoons sour cream
Hot Tomato and Pepper Salsa,
optional (see page 80)

Look for soft flour tortillas in your local supermarket—they warm up quickly on the grill and can be used as an easy way to serve all kinds of roasted vegetables. Simply wrap the chosen filling in a tortilla and eat it. I suggest marinating the corn for 1 hour, but this can be reduced or omitted when time does not allow for marinating.

1 Remove the husks from the corn. Bring a large saucepan of water to a boil and cook the corn for 5 minutes. Drain the ears of corn thoroughly.
2 Mix the catsup, Worcestershire sauce, hot pepper sauce, sugar, and lime juice. Pour over the corn and marinate for 1 hour, turning occasionally.
3 Slice the onion and seed and slice the pepper. Place the corn on the grill rack; grill for 5 to 8 minutes, turning occasionally, until charred and golden. Meanwhile, halve, pit, and skin the avocado. Slice the flesh and toss it in any remaining marinade.
4 Holding the hot corn firmly with a cloth, run a knife down the length of each to remove the kernels. Place kernels in a bowl and mix with the onion, peppers, and avocado.
5 Warm the tortillas for about 2 minutes on the grill. Divide the corn and avocado mixture among the warm tortillas. Place a spoonful of sour cream on top and roll up the tortillas loosely. Serve at once, with Hot Tomato and Pepper Salsa.

Nutrition facts per serving: 430 calories, 19 g total fat (4 g saturated fat), 3 mg cholesterol, 369 mg sodium, 65 g carbohydrate, 8 g fiber, 9 g protein.
Daily values: 14% vitamin A, 69% vitamin C, 7% calcium, 20% iron.

Salads

Any grilled vegetable, tossed with a little good olive oil and a dash of balsamic vinegar, can make an enticing salad. Fortunately, all of the salads in this chapter are quick to prepare and wonderfully fresh. Most of these salads will improve in flavor if you chill them overnight.

COUSCOUS SALAD WITH GRILLED VEGETABLES

Time to prepare: 15 minutes
Time to cook: about 10 minutes

Serves 4

1 ¹/₃ cups couscous

1 ¹/₂ cups cold water or vegetable stock

¹/₄ cup butter

¹/₂ teaspoon ground cinnamon

¹/₂ teaspoon ground ginger

¹/₂ teaspoon paprika

8 shallots

1 eggplant

2 medium zucchini

1 yellow bell pepper

1 garlic clove, minced

1 tablespoon balsamic vinegar

3 tablespoons chopped fresh cilantro

2 tablespoons chopped fresh parsley

salt and freshly ground black pepper

Brushing a spicy butter over the vegetables as they cook gives this salad a wonderful, aromatic sweet-and-sour flavor. Serve it piled into warm pita bread, with Grilled Halloumi Strips (see page 37) for a complete meal that can be eaten without knives and forks.

1 Place the couscous in a bowl and pour in the water or stock. Let stand for 15 minutes, stirring occasionally to break up any lumps.
2 Gently heat the butter and spices together in a small saucepan until melted. Set aside.
3 Place the shallots in a bowl; pour boiling water over shallots and let stand for 5 minutes; then drain and peel. Thread the shallots onto skewers.
4 Thinly slice the eggplant and zucchini lengthwise. Halve and seed the bell pepper. Place the eggplant, bell pepper, and zucchini on the grill rack and brush with the spice butter. Grill the vegetables for 10 minutes, brushing with the spice butter and turning, until they are tender and just blackened.
5 Remove the shallots from the skewers and cut in half. Cut the eggplant, pepper, and zucchini into thin strips.
6 Add the vegetables to the couscous with any remaining butter. Stir in the garlic, balsamic vinegar, cilantro, parsley, and salt and pepper to taste. Serve warm or cold.

Cook's Tip
For a more substantial salad add 1 cup cubed feta or firm goat cheese to the couscous with the grilled vegetables.

Nutrition facts per serving: 393 calories, 12 g total fat (7 g saturated fat), 31 mg cholesterol, 235 mg sodium, 62 g carbohydrate, 13 g fiber, 10 g protein.
Daily values: 40% vitamin A, 72% vitamin C, 4% calcium, 12% iron.

Pouring the remaining spiced butter over the Couscous Salad with Grilled Vegetables

WARM PUY LENTIL SALAD WITH GRILLED EGGPLANT AND FENNEL

Time to prepare: 15 minutes
Time to cook: 35 to 45 minutes
(see recipe introduction)

Serves 4

³/₄ cup Puy lentils
2 fennel bulbs
1 large eggplant
1 red onion
¹/₄ cup pine nuts
1 garlic clove, minced
2 tablespoons chopped fresh mint
1 teaspoon ground cumin
4 tablespoons extra virgin olive oil
1 tablespoon balsamic vinegar
salt and freshly ground black pepper

Puy lentils are the small slate-green legumes that come from the area around the French town of Le Puy. Regarded by chefs as the king of the lentils for their fine texture, smoky flavor, and ability to hold their shape, Puy lentils make a subtle partner for the rich flavors of grilled eggplant and fennel. Start to cook the lentils 15 minutes before putting the vegetables on the grill, and the dish will be ready within 30 minutes in spite of the slightly longer total cooking time.

1 Put the lentils in a saucepan with enough cold water to cover generously. Bring to a boil and simmer for 25 to 30 minutes, until just tender. Drain and place in a salad bowl.
2 Meanwhile, trim the fennel and cut the bulbs into thin slices from tip to root. Cut the stem from the eggplant; cut eggplant into ¹/₂-inch-thick slices. Slice the onion. Toast the pine nuts in a small dry skillet over high heat until golden.
3 Place the fennel and eggplant on the grill rack; grill for 10 to 15 minutes, until browned and tender. Cut the grilled vegetables into thin strips and add them to the warm lentils. Add the onion, pine nuts, and garlic.
4 Mix in the mint, cumin, olive oil, balsamic vinegar, and salt and pepper to taste. Serve at once.

Cook's Tip
Do not substitute red or brown lentils in this dish, as they tend to go mushy. The results will be very disappointing.

Nutrition facts per serving: 352 calories, 20 g total fat (3 g saturated fat), 0 mg cholesterol, 65 mg sodium, 36 g carbohydrate, 15 g fiber, 14 g protein.
Daily values: 1% vitamin A, 19% vitamin C, 5% calcium, 41% iron.

GRILLED BREAD SALAD WITH PARMESAN AND MUSHROOMS

Time to prepare: 10 minutes
Time to cook: 2 to 4 minutes

Serves 4

4 thick slices olive-oil bread or coarse-textured bread
1 garlic clove
3 cups small fresh mushrooms
4 tablespoons chopped fresh flat-leaf parsley
4 tablespoons extra virgin olive oil
1 tablespoon balsamic vinegar
salt and freshly ground black pepper
2-ounce piece Parmesan cheese

Char grilling the bread creates a unique, smoked flavor that marries well with the mild flavor of the mushrooms in this salad.

1 Toast the bread on the grill for 1 to 2 minutes on each side. Cut the garlic clove in half and rub cut side over one side of each slice of bread. Cut the bread into small cubes and place in a salad bowl.
2 Wipe the mushrooms and cut into quarters. Add to the bowl with the parsley. Whisk together the olive oil, vinegar, and salt and pepper to taste; drizzle over the salad.
3 Shave the Parmesan into thin flakes with a vegetable peeler and scatter them over the salad. Lightly toss the ingredients together and serve.

Cook's Tip
This salad can be made with a mixture of mushrooms such as shiitake and oyster mushrooms.

Nutrition facts per serving: 276 calories, 18 g total fat (2 g saturated fat), 10 mg cholesterol, 372 mg sodium, 20 g carbohydrate, 0 g fiber, 9 g protein.
Daily values: 3% vitamin A, 13% vitamin C, 12% calcium, 15% iron.

ARUGULA WITH CHAR-GRILLED RED PEPPER AND CARAMELIZED SHALLOTS

Time to prepare: 10 minutes
Time to cook: 10 to 15 minutes

Serves 4

8 shallots
2 red bell peppers
$1/4$ cup pine nuts
2 ounces feta cheese
$1^1/2$ cups arugula leaves
1 tablespoon red wine vinegar
1 tablespoon light brown sugar
1 tablespoon olive oil plus 2 tablespoons extra virgin olive oil
salt and freshly ground black pepper
Potato and Onion Bread, see page 76 (optional)

The colors of this salad are vibrant and satisfying. Arugula is now available in many supermarkets, in sealed bags or growing in little pots, but it is also incredibly easy to grow, either in a pot or in a small flower bed. It goes to seed rapidly, like spinach, so you have to keep picking it or pinching off the top buds and leaves to keep the plant compact and leafy.

1 Place the shallots in a bowl; pour boiling water over shallots. Let stand for 2 minutes. Drain and peel the shallots and thread them onto skewers. Halve and seed the bell peppers.
2 Toast the pine nuts in a small dry skillet over high heat until golden. Cube the feta. Mix the pine nuts, feta, and arugula in a salad bowl.
3 Mix the vinegar, sugar, and 1 tablespoon olive oil; brush over the shallots and peppers. Place the shallots and peppers on the grill rack; grill for 10 to 15 minutes, brushing with the marinade and turning, until the shallots are golden and the skins of the peppers are blackened.
4 Place the peppers in a plastic bag and set them aside for 5 minutes to loosen their skins. Remove the shallots from the skewers. Peel the peppers and cut them into strips.
5 Arrange the vegetables on the salad. Drizzle with extra virgin olive oil and season to taste with salt and pepper. Toss gently and serve with purchased bread or with the Potato and Onion Bread on page 76.

Nutrition facts per serving: 214 calories, 18 g total fat (4 g saturated fat), 12 mg cholesterol, 198 mg sodium, 11 g carbohydrate, 0 g fiber, 5 g protein.
Daily values: 56% vitamin A, 106% vitamin C, 8% calcium, 10% iron.

ROASTED RATATOUILLE SALAD

Time to prepare: 15 minutes
Time to cook: 15 minutes

Serves 4

1 large eggplant
2 medium zucchini
2 red bell peppers
3 ripe tomatoes
1 large mild onion
4 tablespoons extra virgin olive oil
2 garlic cloves
2 tablespoons red wine vinegar
1 tablespoon capers
salt and freshly ground black pepper
chopped fresh basil, to garnish

Ratatouille can look disappointing if all the vegetables are overcooked and the flavors and textures blend together into a mush. Here, roasting the vegetables keeps their flavors distinct, and the capers and red wine vinegar add a welcome piquancy. This can only be cooked within 30 minutes if you have a very large grill; otherwise, you will have to cook the vegetables in batches.

1 Trim the eggplant and zucchini and slice into thin rounds. Halve and seed the peppers. Halve the tomatoes and onion. Reserve half the olive oil; brush the rest over the vegetables.
2 Place the vegetables on the grill rack; grill for 15 minutes, turning occasionally, until tender and blackened. Place the peppers and tomatoes in a plastic bag and set aside for 5 minutes to loosen their skins. Peel and cut into strips. Slice the onion halves so that the slices separate into strips.
3 Place all the grilled vegetables in a salad bowl. Crush the garlic and add it to the salad. Add the vinegar, capers, salt and pepper to taste, and the remaining olive oil. Scatter with chopped basil and serve at once.

Cook's Tip
This salad makes a tempting topping for a pizza. Spread it over a couple of prepared pizza crusts and scatter some grated mozzarella over the top. Cook for 10 to 12 minutes in a hot oven.

Nutrition facts per serving: 200 calories, 14 g total fat (2 g saturated fat), 0 mg cholesterol, 86 mg sodium, 19 g carbohydrate, 6 g fiber, 3 g protein.
Daily values: 35% vitamin A, 143% vitamin C, 2% calcium, 8% iron.

ROASTED PLUM TOMATOES WITH GARBANZO BEANS

Time to prepare: 15 minutes
Time to cook: 25 to 30 minutes

Serves 4

1 whole head of garlic
1 pound plum tomatoes
14- or 15-ounce can garbanzo beans, drained
1 medium red onion
6 tablespoons chopped fresh basil
4 tablespoons extra virgin olive oil
salt and freshly ground black pepper

Visiting Sicily had a profound effect on the way I cook. The intensity of the flavors, colors, and scents of the island's cuisine has evolved from a diverse cultural heritage—the Moors, Normans, Spanish, and French are just some of the peoples who have conquered the island and moved on, leaving behind their influence, evident in today's culinary style. Couscous, saffron, and spices; fine pastries with almonds and rose water; and a wide selection of superb fruit and vegetables all feature in Sicilian cooking. This salad is a version of one I enjoyed during my stay; it was served with grilled squid and seafood couscous, but it was so good that I could have eaten it on its own, with the local bread to mop up the juices.

1 Wrap the head of garlic in foil and cook it among the coals for 15 to 20 minutes, until tender.
2 Meanwhile, place the tomatoes on the grill rack; grill for about 10 minutes, until the skins blacken. Place in a plastic bag and let stand for 5 minutes to allow the skins to loosen.
3 Meanwhile, place the garbanzo beans in a salad bowl. Slice the onion and add to the garbanzo beans. Add the basil, oil, and salt and pepper to taste.
4 Peel the tomatoes and chop the flesh. Add to the salad and mix well. Squeeze the flesh from the garlic cloves into the salad, mix, and let stand until ready to serve.

Nutrition facts per serving: 245 calories, 15 g total fat (2 g saturated fat), 0 mg cholesterol, 384 mg sodium, 23 g carbohydrate, 6 g fiber, 6 g protein.
Daily values: 7% vitamin A, 48% vitamin C, 5% calcium, 19% iron.

FENNEL AND RED ONION SALAD

Time to prepare: 15 minutes
Time to cook: 10 minutes

Serves 4

2 large fennel bulbs
2 large oranges
1 medium red onion
3 tablespoons extra virgin olive oil
1 tablespoon balsamic vinegar
1 tablespoon chopped fresh mint
salt and freshly ground black pepper
mint, to garnish

Fennel is an ideal vegetable to grill. Cut into thin slices, its strong aniseed flavor mellows as it char grills. As the slices can fall apart, either hold them in place with wooden toothpicks or put them in a grilling basket before placing them on the grill. Juicy oranges and sweet red onions are excellent partners for the fennel. For those who eat fish, this salad goes well with mackerel or tuna.

1 Trim the root ends off the fennel and cut the bulbs into $1/4$-inch-thick slices from tip to root. Place on the grill rack; grill for 5 minutes on each side, turning once, until tender and browned.
2 While the fennel is cooking, carefully peel the oranges with a serrated knife, taking care to remove all the white pith. Cut the flesh into thin slices. Thinly slice the onion.
3 Whisk together the olive oil, balsamic vinegar, mint, and salt and pepper to taste. Layer the fennel in a serving dish with the oranges and onion, drizzling each layer with dressing. Serve at room temperature, garnished with mint.

Cook's Tip
If preparing the fennel in advance, place it in a bowl of water with the juice of $1/2$ lemon to prevent it from discoloring.

Nutrition facts per serving: 136 calories, 10 g total fat (1 g saturated fat), 0 mg cholesterol, 57 mg sodium, 11 g carbohydrate, 13 g fiber, 1 g protein.
Daily values: 1% vitamin A, 53% vitamin C, 3% calcium, 3% iron.

SALAD OF STUFFED PEPPERS WITH TOMATO AND FENNEL

Time to prepare: 10 minutes
Time to cook: about 15 minutes

Serves 4

2 yellow bell peppers
2 red bell peppers
1 medium fennel bulb
8 baby plum or cherry tomatoes
3 tablespoons extra virgin olive oil
salt and freshly ground black pepper
2 tablespoons pesto

Stuffed peppers make a colorful dish that can be served either hot or at room temperature, so they are ideal if your grill rack is getting a little overcrowded, as they can be cooked, then set aside. Securing the stuffing in place with toothpicks ensures that most of it remains in place as the peppers cook, but remember to soak the toothpicks in water first to prevent them from burning.

1 Halve and seed the bell peppers. Cut the fennel into thin slices from tip to root.
2 Place two tomatoes into each pepper half and arrange slices of fennel on top. Secure the fennel in place with a couple of wooden toothpicks placed diagonally across the top of each pepper half. Brush the peppers all over with olive oil and season to taste with salt and pepper.
3 Place the peppers cut sides down on the grill rack; grill for 5 minutes. Turn and continue cooking for about 10 minutes, until the peppers are just charred and tender.
4 Transfer the peppers to a serving dish. Remove the toothpicks and let stand until just cool. When the peppers are still slightly warm, drizzle each one with a little pesto and serve with plenty of bread to mop up any juices.

Cook's Tip
Strict vegetarians can use pesto that has been made with a vegetarian Parmesan, or substitute a good-quality purchased olive paste instead.

Nutrition facts per serving: 177 calories, 15 g total fat (1 g saturated fat), 1 mg cholesterol, 107 mg sodium, 9 g carbohydrate, 6 g fiber, 2 g protein.
Daily values: 30% vitamin A, 232% vitamin C, 1% calcium, 2% iron.

NEW POTATOES AND CAULIFLOWER WITH MINT

Time to prepare: 10 minutes
Time to cook: 15 to 20 minutes

Serves 4

1 pound small new potatoes
1 small head cauliflower
4 tablespoons olive oil
2 tablespoons chopped fresh mint
juice of ½ lemon
salt and freshly ground black pepper
1 teaspoon curry paste

Small new potatoes enlivened with grilled cauliflower dressed with mint transforms potato salad into a meal fit for a king. The hint of spice from good-quality curry paste unites the flavors and textures. Serve in warm naan bread, with a fresh tomato and onion chutney, and yogurt raita.

1 Cook the potatoes in boiling water for 10 to 15 minutes until tender. Meanwhile, cut the cauliflower into flowerets and cook in boiling water for 5 minutes until almost tender. Drain both vegetables and place the potatoes, leaving them whole, in a salad bowl.

2 Whisk together 3 tablespoons of the oil, the mint, lemon juice, and salt and pepper to taste. Pour over the potatoes and toss to coat.

3 Mix the remaining oil with the curry paste. Place the cauliflower flowerets on the grill rack and brush with the flavored oil. Grill for 5 minutes, turning and brushing with more oil. Toss the cauliflower with the potatoes and serve at room temperature.

Cook's Tip
This recipe works without grilling the cauliflower, but do try it this way as the smoky taste imparted by the coals is delicious with the vegetables.

Nutrition facts per serving: 260 calories, 14 g total fat (2 g saturated fat), 0 mg cholesterol, 49 mg sodium, 31 g carbohydrate, 4 g fiber, 5 g protein.
Daily values: 1% vitamin A, 129% vitamin C, 4% calcium, 21% iron.

Breads
and Accompaniments

The breads in this chapter are all incredibly simple to
make and cook, yet they will impress your guests who will
feel that you have made a special effort for them — just the
effect I try to achieve with all my cooking!

POLENTA AND PARMESAN WEDGES

Time to prepare: 15 minutes
Time to cook: 11 to 20 minutes

Serves 4

1/4 **cup pine nuts**

8 black olives, pitted

3 cups water

salt and freshly ground black pepper

generous 1 cup instant polenta

1 tablespoon butter

1/4 **cup freshly grated Parmesan cheese**

3 tablespoons chopped fresh basil

2 tablespoons chopped fresh flat-leaf parsley

2 tablespoons olive oil

Tomato Chili Relish, see page 84, or salsa (optional)

On its own, polenta can be somewhat uninspiring. But here, flavored with Parmesan and fresh herbs and studded with pine nuts and black olives, it becomes something else entirely. And cooking it over coals gives it a delicious, earthy flavor and crisp exterior. Serve these wedges with the Tomato Chili Relish on page 84, or one of the salsas in the Sauces and Relishes chapter.

1 Place the pine nuts in a small skillet and cook over medium heat for 1 to 2 minutes, until golden. Chop the olives. Set both aside.

2 Bring the water to a boil in a large saucepan. Add 1/2 teaspoon salt and pour in the polenta, stirring constantly. Simmer over low heat for 5 to 8 minutes, stirring constantly, until the polenta is thick and coming away from the sides of the pan.

3 Stir the butter, Parmesan, basil, parsley, olives, and toasted pine nuts into the polenta. Season to taste with salt and pepper. Spoon the mixture into a buttered roasting pan and spread it out to a thickness of 1 inch. Cool for 10 minutes, then cut into triangles or wedges.

4 Brush the polenta with olive oil. Place on grill rack; grill for 5 to 10 minutes, turning once or twice, until golden and heated through. Serve with Tomato Chili Relish or salsa.

Nutrition facts per serving: 424 calories, 18 g total fat (4 g saturated fat), 13 mg cholesterol, 187 mg sodium, 56 g carbohydrate, 7 g fiber, 11 g protein.
Daily values: 4% vitamin A, 4% vitamin C, 7% calcium, 12% iron.

Lifting Polenta and Parmesan Wedges off the grill, ready to serve with Tomato Chili Relish

SAGE SHEET BREAD

Time to prepare: 10 minutes
Time to cook: 15 to 20 minutes

Serves 4

1¼ cups all-purpose flour

½ cup fine semolina

1 teaspoon salt

1 tablespoon chopped fresh sage

generous ¾ cup warm water

2 tablespoons extra virgin olive oil

sea salt

Sheet bread originates from Sardinia, where it is also called *Carta da Musica* because it looks like old sheet music. It is simple to prepare and cooks perfectly on the grill, so I make up the dough in advance and cook a few sheets to serve with dips and salsas while the main dishes are grilling.

1 Sift the flour into a large mixing bowl and stir in the semolina, salt, and sage. Pour in the water and mix to a soft dough. Turn the dough onto a floured surface and knead it for 1 minute, adding more flour if the dough gets too sticky.
2 Divide the dough into eight pieces and cover with a damp cloth to prevent it from drying out while you work.
3 Turn out a portion of dough on a floured surface; roll into a very thin circle measuring about 9 inches in diameter.
4 Lay a circle of dough on the grill rack; grill for 1 to 2 minutes on each side, until the surface puffs and bubbles. Brush with olive oil and sprinkle with sea salt while still warm. Continue rolling out and cooking the rest of the dough. Serve the bread warm.

Nutrition facts per serving: 266 calories, 7 g total fat (1 g saturated fat), 0 mg cholesterol, 668 mg sodium, 43 g carbohydrate, 1 g fiber, 6 g protein.
Daily values: 0% vitamin A, 0% vitamin C, 1% calcium, 17% iron.

GARLIC HERB PIZZA BREAD

Time to prepare: 10 minutes
Time to cook: 8 to 10 minutes

Serves 4

1/4 cup butter
2 garlic cloves
2 tablespoons chopped fresh
flat-leaf parsley
salt and freshly ground black
pepper
8-ounce package pizza dough
mix
1 tablespoon extra virgin
olive oil

There are plenty of good pizza-crust mixes available now, and they are ideal for this grilled version of garlic bread. It tastes wonderful, so be sure to make enough to satisfy everyone, especially children.

1 Place the butter in a small bowl and beat until softened. Finely chop the garlic and beat into the butter with the parsley and salt and pepper to taste.
2 Make up the pizza dough mix as instructed on the package, adding the olive oil with the water. Divide the dough in half. Roll out two circles, each about 1/2 inch thick. Do not roll the dough too thin as it will sink through the grill. Use a sharp knife to make about 5 slashes in the top of each dough circle.
3 Lay the dough circles on the well-oiled grill rack. Grill for 4 to 5 minutes on each side, until golden and crisp. Spread the bread with the garlic butter, cut the circles into strips, and serve at once.

Nutrition facts per serving: 336 calories, 17 g total fat (8 g saturated fat), 31 mg cholesterol, 557 mg sodium, 41 g carbohydrate, 0 g fiber, 6 g protein.
Daily values: 11% vitamin A, 5% vitamin C, 0% calcium, 14% iron.

GOAT CHEESE AND DILL BISCUITS

Time to prepare: 10 minutes
Time to cook: 12 to 15 minutes

Makes 10 to 12 biscuits

2 cups self-rising flour
1 teaspoon salt
large pinch cayenne pepper
$1/2$ teaspoon baking powder
2 tablespoons butter
1 tablespoon chopped fresh dill
2 ounces goat cheese
$2/3$ cup plain yogurt
beaten egg to glaze

I serve these oven-baked biscuits topped with spoonfuls of mascarpone and strips of grilled vegetables tossed with a little balsamic vinegar. Use a firm, crumbly goat cheese rather than any of the soft fresh types.

1 Preheat the oven to 400°F. Place a baking sheet in the oven to heat.
2 Sift the flour, salt, cayenne, and baking powder into a large mixing bowl. Cut the butter into dice and rub it into the dry ingredients until the mixture resembles fine bread crumbs. Stir in the dill. Crumble the goat cheese and stir it in. Add the yogurt and mix to a soft dough.
3 Turn the dough onto a lightly floured surface and knead lightly. Roll out to 1 inch thick and use a plain cutter to cut out rounds. Roll out the trimmings and cut more biscuits. Place biscuits on the hot baking sheet and brush the tops with beaten egg.
4 Bake for 12 to 15 minutes, until well risen and golden. Transfer to a wire rack to cool.

Cook's Tip
These biscuits can be made with alternative flavorings; for example, try replacing the dill and goat cheese with basil and feta cheese or sun-dried tomato and mozzarella cheese.

Nutrition facts per serving: 144 calories, 5 g total fat (3 g saturated fat), 33 mg cholesterol, 622 mg sodium, 20 g carbohydrate, 3 g fiber, 5 g protein.
Daily values: 4% vitamin A, 0% vitamin C, 11% calcium, 7% iron.

Goat Cheese and Dill Biscuits topped with mascarpone and grilled vegetables

POTATO AND ONION BREAD

Time to prepare: 15 minutes
Time to cook: 25 minutes

Makes 1 loaf

1 medium mild onion
1 tablespoon olive oil
2 cups bread flour
2 teaspoons baking powder
1 teaspoon salt
$\frac{1}{4}$ teaspoon paprika
1 cup cooked starchy potatoes
1 egg
$\frac{2}{3}$ cup 2% milk
2 tablespoons melted butter
1 teaspoon caraway seeds

This hearty bread makes a wonderful accompaniment for grilled vegetables, particularly sweet varieties such as bell peppers and parsnips. The bread is best when fresh, so make up the dough as soon as the coals are lit. It will cook in half an hour and still be warm and delicious when the rest of your meal is ready.

1 Preheat the oven to 450°F. Finely chop the onion. Heat the oil in a medium skillet and add the onion; cook for 5 minutes, until softened.
2 Meanwhile, sift the flour, baking powder, salt, and paprika into a large mixing bowl. Rub the potatoes into the dry ingredients and stir in the onion.
3 Beat the egg with the milk, stir in the melted butter, and add to the ingredients in the bowl. Mix to a soft dough, which should be quite wet.
4 Turn the dough out onto a well-floured surface and shape it into an 8-inch round. Place on a baking sheet and sprinkle with the caraway seeds. Cut into eight wedges and bake for about 25 minutes, until browned. When the bread is cooked, it will sound hollow when tapped on the base. Serve warm.

Cook's Tip
To make wonderful bruschetta, bake the bread in advance without cutting it into wedges before you cook it. Leave to cool; then cut into thick slices. Place slices on grill rack; grill for 1 minute on each side, until toasted. Moisten with olive oil and serve with the chosen topping, for example, the topping on the Roasted Tomato Crostini on page 12 or on the Charred Green Onion Bruschetta on page 13.

Nutrition facts per serving: 109 calories, 3 g total fat (1 g saturated fat), 18 mg cholesterol, 204 mg sodium, 17 g carbohydrate, 1 g fiber, 3 g protein.
Daily values: 2% vitamin A, 3% vitamin C, 5% calcium, 5% iron.

CINNAMON AND HONEY PANCAKES

Time to prepare: 10 minutes
Time to cook: 15 minutes

Serves 4

2 cups self-rising flour
$^1/_2$ teaspoon ground cinnamon
$^1/_2$ teaspoon cream of tartar
$^1/_4$ teaspoon baking soda
$^1/_4$ teaspoon salt
1 egg
1$^1/_4$ cups milk
2 tablespoons honey
a little sunflower oil for frying
2 tablespoons butter
grilled fruit (optional)

My daughters are avid pancake fans, and it is thanks to them that I discovered how good these pancakes taste when finished on the grill. We reheated the remains of a batch over the fading coals of a summer barbecue and served them with grilled strawberries drizzled with honey. They were wonderful—well worth trying! These pancakes freeze well, so make and freeze a batch if you want to save time. I make the savory version, see below, to serve with char-grilled vegetables and the Salsa Verde on page 85.

1 Sift the flour, cinnamon, cream of tartar, baking soda, and salt into a large mixing bowl. Beat the egg with the milk and honey. Make a well in the center of the dry ingredients, add the liquid, and gradually beat the dry ingredients into the liquid to make a smooth batter.
2 Heat a little oil in a large skillet and spoon a generous tablespoon of the mixture onto the hot surface. Cook for about 2 minutes, until just set and pale golden; then turn and cook the other side. Transfer to a plate. Cook the rest of the mixture in batches.
3 To finish the pancakes, melt the butter in a small pan and brush over the pancakes. Place them on the grill rack and heat through on both sides. Serve with grilled fruit.

Savory Pancakes
For savory pancakes, omit the cinnamon and honey from the recipe and add chopped fresh herbs to the batter. Snipped chives, chopped thyme, and/or tarragon are suitable.

Nutrition facts per serving: 391 calories, 12 g total fat (5 g saturated fat), 74 mg cholesterol, 1,117 mg sodium, 59 g carbohydrate, 8 g fiber, 10 g protein.
Daily values: 12% vitamin A, 1% vitamin C, 26% calcium, 19% iron.

Sauces and Relishes

Well-flavored sauces are essential for grilling: they provide welcome moisture and add zest to bland foods or a dash of color and texture where needed. Serve them to enhance, but not overpower, the main ingredients.

ROMESCO SAUCE

Time to prepare: 10 minutes
Time to cook: 10 to 17 minutes

Serves 4

1 medium onion
3 garlic cloves
2 red bell peppers
4 ripe tomatoes
$1/2$ cup blanched almonds or hazelnuts
1 large red chili pepper
2 tablespoons red wine vinegar
$1/2$ cup extra virgin olive oil
salt and freshly ground black pepper

This stunning yet simple sauce based on roasted vegetables and nuts comes from the Tarragona region of Spain, where it is traditionally served with grilled shellfish. Grill the peppers and tomatoes to make a wonderfully smoky sauce that can be used as a dip or relish. It can even be poured over pasta.

1 Halve the onion horizontally. Thread the garlic onto a wooden skewer.
2 Place the onion, garlic, whole peppers, and tomatoes on the grill rack; grill for 8 to 15 minutes, turning often, until the skins are charred. (The garlic and tomatoes will cook faster and should be removed from the grill first.)
3 Place the peppers and tomatoes in a plastic bag and set aside for 5 minutes to allow the skins to loosen.
4 Peel and seed the peppers and tomatoes, catching any juice. Roughly chop the flesh and place in a blender or food processor with any juice.
5 Fry the almonds or hazelnuts in a small skillet without oil for about 2 minutes, until golden. Add to the tomato mixture and process to a paste. Chop and seed the chili pepper. Add the chili pepper, garlic, and onion to the sauce.
6 With the motor running, slowly pour in the vinegar and olive oil; then continue to process until the sauce is smooth. Season to taste with salt and pepper; let stand at room temperature until ready to serve.

Cook's Tip
Store any extra sauce in a covered container in the refrigerator for up to a week. Bring the sauce to room temperature before it is served to allow the flavors to develop.

Nutrition facts per serving: 382 calories, 36 g total fat (4 g saturated fat), 0 mg cholesterol, 48 mg sodium, 15 g carbohydrate, 4 g fiber, 5 g protein.
Daily values: 35% vitamin A, 164% vitamin C, 5% calcium, 10% iron.

Dry-frying almonds ready for Romesco Sauce

HOT TOMATO AND PEPPER SALSA

Time to prepare: 10 minutes

Serves 4

3 ripe plum tomatoes

1 to 2 green chili peppers

1 yellow bell pepper

1 small red onion

2 tablespoons chopped fresh basil

1 tablespoon red wine vinegar

1/4 cup olive oil

salt and freshly ground black pepper

Tomatoes, chili peppers, and bell peppers make the perfect base for salsas, but you can vary the ingredients as you wish—just aim for a balance of textures, colors, and flavors. Take this basic recipe as a starter and move on. This is a fiery version; for a milder taste, try the Avocado, Mango, and Lime Salsa on page 82.

1 Quarter, seed, and chop the tomatoes. Seed and finely chop the chili peppers and bell pepper. Finely chop the red onion.

2 Place all the prepared vegetables in a bowl and add the basil, wine vinegar, and olive oil. Season to taste with salt and pepper and mix well. Cover; chill until ready to serve.

Variations

AVOCADO, TOMATO, AND PEPPER SALSA Add the diced flesh of 1 ripe avocado with juice of 1 lime instead of the vinegar.

ROASTED PEPPER AND HOT TOMATO SALSA Place the yellow bell pepper and 1 red bell pepper on the grill rack; grill until the skin is blackened. Place in a plastic bag and set aside for 5 minutes to allow the skins to loosen; skin and seed the peppers. Chop the flesh and add to the salsa. Use balsamic vinegar instead of red wine vinegar, and use 1/2 green chili pepper instead of the whole chili pepper. Use the best extra virgin olive oil in this version, which makes an excellent topping for bruschetta.

CUCUMBER AND CILANTRO SALSA Replace the basil with chopped fresh cilantro and omit the yellow pepper. Fry 1 teaspoon cumin seeds in a skillet without oil for 30 seconds; add to the salsa with 3/4 cup diced cucumber.

Nutrition facts per serving: 142 calories, 14 g total fat (2 g saturated fat), 0 mg cholesterol, 40 mg sodium, 5 g carbohydrate, 1 g fiber, 1 g protein.
Daily values: 4% vitamin A, 86% vitamin C, 0% calcium, 2% iron.

PEANUT SATAY SAUCE

Time to prepare: 5 minutes
Time to cook: 8 minutes

Serves 4

1 small onion
1 tablespoon olive oil
1 dried chili pepper
2 tablespoons dark soy sauce
juice of 1 lime
1 tablespoon light brown sugar
8 tablespoons crunchy peanut butter
²/₃ cup coconut milk
salt

This peanut butter sauce is one of my favorite recipes for cooking the humble groundnut (an alternative name reflecting the fact that peanuts grow on the ground). The sauce is based on a recipe I was given years ago in the South Pacific, and it goes well with any Asian-inspired kabobs such as the Vegetable Satay on page 30.

1 Finely chop the onion. Heat the oil in a small saucepan and add the onion; cook over medium heat for about 5 minutes, until softened. Turn up the heat and continue cooking for about 2 minutes, until golden.
2 Crush the chili pepper and add it to the saucepan. Cook for 30 seconds more. Add the soy sauce, lime juice, and sugar. Remove from the heat.
3 Stir in the peanut butter; then add enough coconut milk to give the sauce a thick pouring consistency. Season to taste with salt. Serve as a sauce or dip.

Cook's Tip
You can store this sauce in a screw-topped jar in the refrigerator for up to one month. Do not add the coconut milk until just before serving. To use, simply heat gently and add enough coconut milk to give the correct consistency.

Nutrition facts per serving: 316 calories, 27 g total fat (10 g saturated fat), 0 mg cholesterol, 721 mg sodium, 14 g carbohydrate, 2 g fiber, 9 g protein.
Daily values: 3% vitamin A, 4% vitamin C, 1% calcium, 9% iron.

AVOCADO, MANGO, AND LIME SALSA

Time to prepare: 10 minutes

Serves 4

1 large ripe avocado
1 large ripe mango
6 green onions
juice of 1 lime
2 tablespoons chopped fresh mint
$1/2$ teaspoon mild curry paste
salt and freshly ground black pepper

Serve the salsa with naan bread and the Sweet Potatoes with Quick Curry Paste, on page 56.

1 Halve, pit, and skin the avocado. Dice the flesh and place it in a mixing bowl. Peel the mango, cut the flesh away from the pit, and dice it. Thinly slice the green onions. Add the green onions and mango to the avocado.
2 Mix the lime juice, mint, curry paste, and salt and pepper to taste. Pour over the fruit and mix well. Serve at once.

Nutrition facts per serving: 128 calories, 8 g total fat (1 g saturated fat), 0 mg cholesterol, 42 mg sodium, 16 g carbohydrate, 4 g fiber, 2 g protein.
Daily values: 33% vitamin A, 47% vitamin C, 2% calcium, 10% iron.

CUCUMBER AND WALNUT RAITA

Time to prepare: 10 minutes

Serves 4

$1/4$ small cucumber
$1/4$ cup walnut pieces
$1^1/4$ cups plain yogurt
1 teaspoon cumin seeds
few drops bottled hot pepper sauce
2 tablespoons lemon juice
3 tablespoons chopped fresh cilantro or mint
salt and freshly ground black pepper

I serve this recipe with practically every savory dish I grill on the barbecue.

1 Finely dice the cucumber and chop the walnut halves. Place the yogurt in a mixing bowl and stir in the cucumber and walnuts.
2 Fry cumin seeds in a skillet without oil 30 seconds. Using a mortar and pestle, grind to a powder. Add to the yogurt.
3 Stir the hot pepper sauce, lemon juice, cilantro or mint, and salt and pepper to taste into the yogurt mixture. Cover and chill before serving.

Nutrition facts per serving: 100 calories, 6 g total fat (1 g saturated fat), 4 mg cholesterol, 153 mg sodium, 8 g carbohydrate, 1 g fiber, 5 g protein.
Daily values: 2% vitamin A, 9% vitamin C, 12% calcium, 4% iron.

Avocado, Mango, and Lime Salsa served with Sweet Potatoes with Quick Curry Paste and naan bread

TOMATO CHILI RELISH

Time to prepare: 5 minutes
Time to cook: 20 to 25 minutes

Serves 4

1½ pounds ripe plum tomatoes or 1¾-pound can Italian plum tomatoes

2 mild red chili peppers (use hot if you prefer a fiery flavor)

3 garlic cloves

⅓ cup brown sugar

4 tablespoons chopped fresh basil

salt

Brush this catsup-like relish over vegetables or tofu as they cook over the coals or serve a little of the relish with kabobs or grilled root vegetables. Use fresh tomatoes only if they are really full of flavor; otherwise, use canned Italian plum tomatoes for the correct intensity. Canned tomatoes also have the advantage of being quick to prepare, whereas fresh produce has to be peeled before use.

1 If using fresh tomatoes, peel and chop them. Place the tomatoes, chili peppers, and garlic in a blender or food processor. Process until smooth. Sieve the mixture into a large saucepan, pressing through as much as you can.
2 Stir in the sugar and cook over a gentle heat until it dissolves. Bring the relish to a boil and simmer for 20 to 25 minutes, until thickened. Stir in the basil and salt to taste. Serve hot or cold.

Nutrition facts per serving: 86 calories, 0 g total fat (0 g saturated fat), 0 mg cholesterol, 49 mg sodium, 21 g carbohydrate, 2 g fiber, 1 g protein.
Daily values: 7% vitamin A, 65% vitamin C, 2% calcium, 6% iron.

SALSA VERDE

Time to prepare: 5 minutes

Serves 4

1 to 2 garlic cloves

1 tablespoon capers

1 small red onion

6 tablespoons chopped fresh flat-leaf parsley

4 tablespoons extra virgin olive oil

salt and freshly ground black pepper

Parsley and garlic are the essential ingredients for this, the simplest and probably the most versatile recipe in the book. I recommend flat-leaf rather than curly parsley for its strong flavor and the very best extra virgin olive oil. Use the salsa as a marinade or to brush over practically any vegetables as they cook on the grill. Spread it over toasted bread for the simplest bruschetta. Non-vegetarians can try this salsa spooned over mussels or any grilled fish and meat.

1 Finely chop the garlic, capers, and onion. Place in a small bowl and stir in the parsley, oil, and salt and pepper to taste.

Nutrition facts per serving: 128 calories, 14 g total fat (2 g saturated fat), 0 mg cholesterol, 75 mg sodium, 2 g carbohydrate, 0 g fiber, 0 g protein.
Daily values: 2% vitamin A, 14% vitamin C, 1% calcium, 3% iron.

Desserts

I tend to run out of time and hot coals when
it comes to adding the finishing touch to a successful
barbecue. Since creating these quick-fix dessert recipes, I
keep the coals hot as the barbecue progresses in order to
cook a selection of fruit which is so well suited to this
cooking method.

BANANA AND STRAWBERRY KABOBS WITH STICKY TOFFEE SAUCE

Time to prepare: 15 minutes
Time to cook: 5 to 8 minutes

Serves 4

2 tablespoons butter
1 tablespoon honey
¹/₄ teaspoon ground cinnamon
3 large bananas
1¹/₂ cups strawberries

Sticky Toffee Sauce
²/₃ cup light brown sugar
4 tablespoons whipping cream
¹/₄ cup butter
few drops vanilla extract

Bananas could have been designed for the grill. One of my standby finales to round off a meal cooked over the coals involves cooking bananas in their skins on the grill, turning them until they are blackened. Then the skin is cut open and spoonfuls of honey, rum, and cream are poured in so that the lucky recipient can scoop out a combination of all the flavors at once—this is incredibly simple and completely sublime! These kabobs are only slightly more time consuming to prepare, and they are just as delicious.

1 Melt the 2 tablespoons butter with the honey and cinnamon. Skin the bananas and cut them into thick slices at a slant. Thread the slices onto skewers with the strawberries and brush with the melted butter mixture.
2 Make the sauce before cooking the kabobs. Combine the sugar, cream, and remaining butter in a small saucepan. Heat until melted. Simmer for 5 minutes, until thickened. Stir in the vanilla extract. Set the sauce aside.
3 Place the kabobs on the grill rack; grill for 5 to 8 minutes, turning occasionally and brushing with the butter, until the bananas turn golden.
4 Serve the kabobs at once with the warm Sticky Toffee Sauce poured over.

Nutrition facts per serving: 425 calories, 23 g total fat (14 g saturated fat), 66 mg cholesterol, 190 mg sodium, 58 g carbohydrate, 3 g fiber, 2 g protein.
Daily values: 23% vitamin A, 65% vitamin C, 4% calcium, 8% iron.

Ladling Sticky Toffee Sauce over
Banana and Strawberry Kabobs

EXOTIC FRUIT KABOBS WITH CARDAMOM RUM BUTTER

Time to prepare: 15 minutes
Time to cook: 5 to 8 minutes

Serves 4

¹/₂ **small pineapple**

1 ripe mango

¹/₂ **papaya**

Cardamom Rum Butter

¹/₄ **cup butter**

4 cardamom pods

¹/₂ **teaspoon freshly ground black pepper**

2 tablespoons light brown sugar

2 tablespoons dark rum or sweet sherry

Black pepper really brings out the flavors of some fruits; many people sprinkle it on strawberries for just that reason. Here pepper is combined with fragrant cardamom in a wonderful glaze brushed on exotic fruits.

1 Peel the pineapple and cut it into thick slices. Remove the hard core and cut the fruit into bite-sized chunks. Peel the mango, cut the flesh away from the pit, and cut it into chunks. Halve and seed the papaya, peel it, and cut it into chunks. Thread the fruit onto skewers.

2 Place the butter in a small saucepan. Crush the cardamom pods and scrape out the tiny black seeds into the pan. Add the pepper, sugar, and rum or sherry. Heat gently until melted; brush over the fruit.

3 Place the kabobs on the grill rack; grill for 5 to 8 minutes, turning occasionally, until the fruit is golden. Serve at once.

Nutrition facts per serving: 216 calories, 12 g total fat (7 g saturated fat), 31 mg cholesterol, 120 mg sodium, 26 g carbohydrate, 2 g fiber, 1 g protein.
Daily values: 34% vitamin A, 62% vitamin C, 2% calcium, 4% iron.

GRILLED PEACHES WITH WHISKEY MAC CREAM

Time to prepare: 15 minutes
Time to marinate: 1 hour
Time to cook: 5 minutes

Serves 4

4 large ripe peaches

1 tablespoon grated fresh gingerroot

$^1/_2$ teaspoon ground cinnamon

$^2/_3$ cup ginger wine

Whiskey Mac Cream

3 ounces mascarpone or cream cheese

$^2/_3$ cup whipping cream

2 tablespoons whiskey

1 tablespoon superfine sugar

grated peel of $^1/_2$ lemon

Ginger wine partnered with whiskey (the whiskey mac) is one of my family's cures for a cold. It also makes an excellent marinade for fruit. The peaches need to be marinated in the spiced ginger wine for about 1 hour.

1 Pour boiling water over the peaches in a colander and leave for 1 minute. Drain and skin the peaches; halve them and remove their pits.

2 Place the peach halves in a shallow dish and scatter with the grated gingerroot and cinnamon. Pour the ginger wine over the mixture; cover and marinate in the refrigerator for about 1 hour.

3 To make the whiskey mac cream, place the mascarpone or cream cheese in a bowl and beat until softened. Lightly whip the cream; fold the cream, whiskey, sugar, and lemon peel into the mascarpone. Stir in 2 tablespoons of the ginger wine from the peaches.

4 Drain the peaches and place on the grill rack. Grill for about 5 minutes, turning to cook evenly, and serve with the whiskey mac cream.

Cook's Tip
Other fruit can be prepared using this marinade; pineapple and mango are both ideal.

Nutrition facts per serving: 360 calories, 25 g total fat (15 g saturated fat), 82 mg cholesterol, 29 mg sodium, 25 g carbohydrate, 3 g fiber, 6 g protein.
Daily values: 26% vitamin A, 19% vitamin C, 3% calcium, 2% iron.

PEACH AND BLUEBERRY PARCELS WITH PECAN BUTTER

Time to prepare: 10 minutes
Time to cook: 10 minutes

Serves 4

4 ripe peaches
2 cups blueberries
¼ cup pecan halves
¼ cup butter
3 tablespoons light brown sugar
1 teaspoon ground cinnamon
4 tablespoons dark rum
whipped cream (optional)

The combination of peaches and blueberries is one of summer's age-old delights. Here they are cooked in a divine sweet-buttery sauce. As you can imagine, all kinds of ripe fruit can be substituted for those suggested in this recipe.

1 Halve and pit the peaches. Mix with the blueberries. Place the pecans in a small saucepan and cook over medium heat for 1 to 2 minutes, until toasted. Finely chop the pecans. Beat the butter with the sugar and cinnamon until soft and light; then beat in the pecans.
2 Cut four 10-inch-square sheets of foil and divide the fruit among them. Dot with the cinnamon butter and sprinkle each with 1 tablespoon rum. Fold the edges of the foil and twist them to seal in the fruit.
3 Place packets on grill rack; grill for 10 minutes, until the fruit starts to soften. Open the foil packages and serve with whipped cream.

Cook's Tip
These foil-wrapped fruit packages can also be cooked in the oven, making them an excellent make-ahead dessert for dinner parties.

Nutrition facts per serving: 323 calories, 16 g total fat (7 g saturated fat), 31 mg cholesterol, 123 mg sodium, 39 g carbohydrate, 5 g fiber, 2 g protein.
Daily values: 20% vitamin A, 34% vitamin C, 2% calcium, 5% iron.

FIGS WITH LEMON GRASS AND HONEY

Time to prepare: 5 minutes
Time to cook: 5 to 8 minutes

Serves 4

8 ripe figs
4 tablespoons good-quality honey
1 stem lemon grass
$^1/_4$ cup walnut pieces

I love figs. I first sampled them picked from trees growing in the orchard around the pool of our Spanish holiday villa. Grilling was an everyday method of cooking the wonderful fresh ingredients from the local markets. Toward the end of a meal we would place figs on the rack to cook gently in the last heat of the dying embers. Drizzled with local honey and eaten with local fresh cheese, they were the perfect way to end a summer meal.

1 Place the figs on the grill rack; grill for 5 to 8 minutes, until the skins start to blacken. Use tongs to turn the figs carefully as they cook, without piercing their skins. Arrange on serving plates.
2 Gently warm the honey and lemon grass in a small saucepan. Remove the lemon grass and pour the honey over the figs. Sprinkle with walnuts and serve.

Nutrition facts per serving: 191 calories, 5 g total fat (0 g saturated fat), 0 mg cholesterol, 4 mg sodium, 38 g carbohydrate, 7 g fiber, 2 g protein.
Daily values: 1% vitamin A, 3% vitamin C, 3% calcium, 4% iron.

LEMON-GLAZED PEARS ON RAISIN TOAST

Time to prepare: 15 minutes
Time to cook: 10 minutes

Serves 4

2 tablespoons butter
grated peel and juice of
¹/₂ lemon
2 tablespoons superfine sugar
4 large ripe pears
4 slices cinnamon raisin bread
4 tablespoons mascarpone or
cream cheese

My sister tested the recipes for this book, and this was one of her favorites. She said that the raisin bread was so delicious toasted on the grill and spread with mascarpone that she almost forgot to add the pears! Look for mascarpone cheese at your supermarket or an Italian market.

1 Place the butter, lemon peel and juice, and sugar in a small saucepan. Heat gently until melted.
2 Peel, halve, and core the pears. Brush the lemon glaze over the pears. Place on the grill rack; grill for 5 to 8 minutes, turning occasionally, until golden brown.
3 While the pears are cooking, toast the bread on both sides on the grill rack. Spread one side with the mascarpone or cream cheese and top each slice with two cooked pear halves. Serve at once.

Nutrition facts per serving: 227 calories, 10 g total fat (6 g saturated fat), 24 mg cholesterol, 163 mg sodium, 34 g carbohydrate, 2 g fiber, 4 g protein.
Daily values: 5% vitamin A, 12% vitamin C, 2% calcium, 6% iron.

RASPBERRY AND RED CURRANT FOOL

Time to prepare: 15 minutes

Serves 4 to 6

1 pound fresh raspberries
1 cup red currants
6 tablespoons superfine sugar
1¼ cups whipping cream
⅔ cup plain yogurt

Decoration
raspberries
bunches of red currants

I make a lot of fruit fools during the summer, starting with rhubarb and gooseberry and moving on to red berries. Quick to make but always popular, they are an ideal dessert to follow a grilled main course. I serve ginger cookies with the fool—homemade if I have time or purchased if I don't. Any leftover fool can be frozen to make the simplest ice cream.

1 Mash the raspberries and red currants together with a fork until fairly smooth but not puréed. Stir in the sugar.
2 Lightly whip the cream to soft peaks (tips curl); stir in the yogurt. Fold in the fruit mixture, but do not overmix: the fool should have a slightly marbled effect.
3 Spoon the mixture into individual serving glasses and decorate with a few raspberries and bunches of currants.

Cook's Tip
This recipe works well using other summer berries such as strawberries or blackberries.

Nutrition facts per serving: 425 calories, 29 g total fat (18 g saturated fat), 104 mg cholesterol, 55 mg sodium, 40 g carbohydrate, 6 g fiber, 5 g protein.
Daily values: 35% vitamin A, 67% vitamin C, 12% calcium, 6% iron.

ALMOND STUFFED APRICOTS

Time to prepare: 15 minutes
Time to cook: 5 to 10 minutes

Serves 4

1 pound ripe apricots
a little melted butter

Stuffing
$^1/_2$ cup blanched almonds
2 tablespoons superfine sugar
1 egg yolk
1 tablespoon brandy or kirsch
mascarpone or cream cheese, ice cream, or yogurt, to serve (optional)

In this sumptuous but simple recipe, pitted apricots are stuffed with a frangipane cream made from ground almonds and threaded onto pairs of skewers. Brushed with butter or left plain, they grill perfectly on the barbecue. Serve with mascarpone or cream cheese and a glass of wine for a great finish to a summer meal; the fat-conscious can opt for yogurt.

1 Halve the apricots and remove the pits. Grind the almonds in a blender or food processor until finely ground, but don't over-process, as the nuts will turn oily.
2 Transfer the nuts to a small bowl and stir in the sugar, egg yolk, and liqueur until a stiff paste forms. Spoon a little of the paste into the center of each apricot half and put the halves back together to form a whole fruit.
3 Thread the stuffed apricots onto thin metal skewers, using two for each to hold the fruit together. (Place four or five apricots on each skewer.) Brush the fruit with melted butter if desired.
4 Place the skewers on the grill rack; grill for 5 to 10 minutes, turning often, until the apricots are tender and cooked through. Serve at once with mascarpone or cream cheese, ice cream, or yogurt.

Nutrition facts per serving: 223 calories, 13 g total fat (3 g saturated fat), 61 mg cholesterol, 34 mg sodium, 22 g carbohydrate, 4 g fiber, 6 g protein.
Daily values: 40% vitamin A, 19% vitamin C, 5% calcium, 9% iron.

INDEX